91
FEET

91 FEET

"You're Privileged to See a Dangerous Shark"

Lee E. Pate

iUniverse, Inc.
New York Lincoln Shanghai

91 FEET

"You're Privileged to See a Dangerous Shark"

iUniverse books may be ordered through booksellers or by contacting:

iUniverse
2021 Pine Lake Road, Suite 100
Lincoln, NE 68512
www.iuniverse.com
1-800-Authors (1-800-288-4677)

ISBN: 978-0-595-42939-4 (pbk)
ISBN: 978-0-595-87281-7 (ebk)

Printed in the United States of America

Many thanks to my wife Sherry,
for all of your help and support.
Your contribution is deeply appreciated.

Contents

Chapter 1 The lesson 1
Chapter 2 Diving on our own 47
Chapter 3 Night diving 75
Chapter 4 Redondo Canyon 95
Chapter 5 You're Privileged to See a Dangerous Shark 129

Chapter 1

The lesson

It's a nice hot day just right for a water skiing trip to the lake. Everything was packed in the boat except for the water skis. I was carrying to the boat. The boat is a seventeen-foot tri-hull with an open bow and an eighty-five horsepower outboard motor. I cut the railing off the front of it and put anti skid strips on it so we can walk up and stand on the front and dive off into the water.

I put the skis in the boat. I'm going to wait to put the cover on the boat in case Deb and Scott needs to put anything inside it first. Deb is my sister and Scott is her husband. Deb and I both work shift work but Deb is also taking college classes. She was working on getting her degree. Scott worked the day shift. They have a pickup that can haul the boat without any trouble. I only have a little car that can barely make it on its own much less haul a boat around.

I could hear their pickup. I looked down the long driveway of the duplex I lived in. I lived in the back house. It was a small one-bedroom house but was big enough for me. Scott was backing up toward the boat. I walked over to the boat and started guiding him back.

Scott backed up close to the trailer. I started cranking the trailer down onto Scott's trailer hitch. Deb and Scott got out and walked back to where I was. Scott plugged the light connector together. I said, "Do you guys have anything to put in the boat?" Scott said, "No, it all fit in the truck." I said, "Let's get the boat cover on and hit the road then." Scott said okay then he looked at Deb and said, "Hon will you fill up my glass with diet soda while we put on the boat cover and get the dogs." Deb said, "Sure Hon." Scott and I tied down the boat cover.

Scott loaded the dogs in the back of the pickup. I'm not really a dog person but these are pretty good dogs. There's Dusty that's always ready to go and all perky and energetic then there's Sam. Both dogs are pretty big but Sam is afraid of everything even a fly. He doesn't think he's safe unless he's at home even then he's not really sure.

We all got in the truck. We were on the way to the lake. I looked back and checked the trailer. Everything looked good but I always worried about the trailer. It was getting old. I should replace it but hopefully it'll last for a few more trips.

We started talking about skiing and how much fun we're going to have. We like the water and try to go skiing and swimming every chance we get. Deb said, "I'm thinking about signing up for scuba diving lessons when we get back." I said, "That sounds like fun, sign me up too and I'll do them with you." Scott started looking at me and started giggling and smiling. I think he didn't really think she would do it. You always hear about how tough you have to be in order to scuba dive.

We went up to the lake, camped and water-skied for two days then went back home. Scott backed the boat up and parked it then Deb and Scott went home.

The next day …

Deb called and said, "There's a scuba diving place not far from our houses." I said, "I don't know anything about diving but that sounds okay with me. How can you take lessons unless you're in the water?" Deb said, "Yeah that's right. I'll call them and find out."

Deb called back and said, "You do the classroom work at the dive shop on Tuesday and Thursday and the dive training at the beach on Saturday and Sunday. You just walk right into the water at the beach and go diving. If you complete all the training you can be certified in two weeks." I said, "Wow, that's fast. It sounds like fun." Deb said, "I know. Do you want to go talk to them?" I said, "Yeah, I'll come and pick you up." Deb said, "Okay."

I drove over and picked Deb up. We drove to the dive shop and walked in. There was a worker behind the counter. He said, "Hello I'm Eddie can I help you." Deb said, "Yeah, I'm the one that called earlier." Eddie said, "I remember you." Deb said, "We want to sign up for scuba diving lessons." Eddie said, "Okay come with me."

We walked over to a shelf that had some books on it. Eddie picked up a big blue cloth envelope with a zipper on it, unzipped it, pulled out some papers and a book. Eddie said, "You'll need to fill these out and start reading this book." He was showing us the papers and the book. He said, "Read as much as you can of the book before the class. The classes start every other Tuesday. So you can start this Tuesday if you would like." Deb and I both said, "We do - we'll be here Tuesday." Eddie said, "Okay I'll sign you guys up. You'll need a mask, snorkel, booties and fins. We furnish everything else." Deb and I started looking at the mask and snorkels. Eddie said, "It's easier if you get a mask and snorkel with a drain that way you just blow and the water drains out." Deb and I started looking at the mask and snorkels with drains. We found the ones we liked. We walked over to the booties and started looking at them, they were easy to pick out - just find your size. We walked over and started looking at the fins. Eddie pointed at some and said, "These are the ones I like. But you can get these big ones or those little ones. The little ones are really easy to use. You just won't go very fast. The big ones go fast but they take a lot of energy." I said, "I'll take the ones like you've got." Deb said, "I'll take these little ones."

Eddie was really funny and kept joking around with us. Deb and I paid for our stuff then Eddie said, "Come on I'll show you around." Deb and I followed him. Eddie pointed in a room and said, "This is the classroom." We followed him into the classroom. It's a little room with a table and chairs around it and a TV at the end of the table on a TV stand with a VCR under it. On the wall to the side of the table is a dry erase board. We looked around, then walked out and over to the next room where the back door was. Eddie said, "This is the filling area where we fill the tanks." We looked around at the equipment then walked back to the front of the dive shop.

Eddie said, "It's so much fun diving. My son and I go all the time." Deb said, "It sounds like fun." Another customer walked in. Eddie walked over to them and started helping them. Deb and I looked around a little more then decided to leave. I looked over at Eddie and waved and said, "We'll see you Tuesday." Eddie waved back and said "Okay." I drove Deb back home and dropped her off then drove home.

Tuesday ...

It's finally Tuesday and time to go to our first dive class. I didn't think it would ever be time to go. It reminded me of waiting for Christmas when I was a kid.

I called Deb and asked, "You ready?" Deb said, "Yeah, come pick me up." I said, "Okay I'm on my way." I drove over to Deb's house and picked her up then drove to the dive shop. We were all excited. I felt like a school kid again. We had our book, pen and papers. We parked in front of the dive shop and walked in. We were a little early so we started looking around the dive shop. A young lady walked in and started looking around too.

After a few minutes a guy walked out from the back, looked at me, Deb and the young lady. He said, "Hello I'm Ron. I'll be your instructor." All three of us said hello. Ron said, "We're almost ready to start. Come on back." He turned around and started walking to the classroom. We all followed him.

We sat down at the table. Ron looked at Deb and said, "Do you go by Deb or Debbie?" Deb said, "Deb" then Ron looked at the young lady. She said, "Debbie." Ron said, "Good" then he looked at me. I said, "Lee." Ron said, "Deb, Debbie and Lee."

Ron said, "What we'll do on all four of the classroom days is watch a movie, go over the book, have a discussion time and on the last day, have a small test. Is everyone ready to start? We all started shaking our heads yes. Ron said, "Good. Let's get started." Ron walked over to the TV and VCR and turned them on then walked over and dimmed the lights. The video started …

This video is part one of four of the training videos. We hope you enjoy the video. We'll start with what most of you are all ready familiar with - the mask and snorkel.

Masks are all about the same. About the only difference are the extras you can get with it such as a drain. With a drain you can breathe out of your nose and drain any water that has gotten into your mask. While underwater your mask will be a little bit deceiving because it makes things twenty five percent closer and thirty three percent larger. So if you're going to touch something it might be a little further away and a little smaller than it looks. That soda can you see will look like a jumbo size can.

The snorkel is fairly simple. It's just a tube that you breathe through while you're on the surface. You can use it to breathe with while looking down and trying to find a place that you want to go diving at. People that aren't divers usually put it on the right side of their head, but you can always tell a diver because they put it on the left side. That way, when they find the place they want to go down at they simply take their snorkel out of their mouth and put in their regulator and go down.

Next will be gloves. Gloves are similar to the gloves you wear when you're in the snow. They're mainly to keep your hands warm but they also protect your hands from being scraped or cut. They're usually thick and bulky so you don't want to put them on until you're close to getting in the water. It's hard to buckle a buckle or snap a snap with gloves on.

Next will be the fins. There are mainly two types of fins. The shoe type and the open heel type. The shoe type is mainly used where the water is warm so you just slip your bare feet into them. The open heel type you wear with booties and are mainly used in cooler water.

The booties are just like what they sound like. They're like a high top shoe and most of them have a tread on the bottom so you can walk around when you're out of the water. Their main purpose is to keep your feet warm while diving.

Next is the wetsuit. The wetsuit is a suit made of neoprene or a similar substance. When you get into the water it lets in a small amount of water that your body warms up fairly quick. It's that initial soaking that's chilly. The thicker the neoprene the better it keeps the water in so the warmer it keeps you.

There are one-piece wetsuits and two-piece farmer john type wetsuits. On a one piece the body, legs and arms are all made to be one piece. On two piece farmer john type wetsuits you have an overall type pants and a jacket type top. That way, if you have a six millimeter farmer john wetsuit it covers your body with both the overall pants and the jacket giving you two layers. So if you have a six-millimeter farmer john wetsuit it makes the area over your torso twelve millimeters thick.

There is also another kind of wetsuit called a drysuit. You really do stay dry in it but most people use a wetsuit, especially new divers.

Next is the hood. The hood is very important because without a hood. You'll loose a lot of body heat out from your head causing you to be extremely cold. A hood just slides over your head and neck then extends down into your wetsuit a few inches. There are also hooded vests. That instead of extending down into your wetsuit a few inches it's actually a hood with a vest attached. So just like the farmer john wetsuit, the vest will add additional thickness to make you even warmer.

Up to here we've covered the mask, snorkel, gloves, fins, booties, wetsuit and hood. Now let's work on your buoyancy compensator or BC, weights, tank, regulators, gauges, compass, timing device or watch, whistle, dive light and dive knife.

The buoyancy compensator or BC has three purposes 1) to act somewhat like a life jacket to just hold your head above water and 2) to keep you neutral at whatever depth you're at and 3) control your descent rate down and ascent rate up.

The BC is like a backpack with a balloon or bladder that will hold air. Just air it up and it acts like a life jacket so you can float on the surface, snorkel around, turn over on your back and kick in or out to your diving location or your exit location.

As you descend down the increased pressure will cause your wetsuit, dive gear and the air in your BC to compress causing you to not have as much floatation. You'll need to add air to your BC to control your descending rate going down or to become neutral once you get to the depth you want to stay at. The reverse is true ascending up; your wetsuit, dive gear and the air in your BC will be expanding causing you to have too much floatation. You'll need to release air from your BC to control your ascending rate going up.

The BC also has a safety valve or dump valve mounted on it. This valve is to protect the BC bladder from rupturing by being overfilled with air. If the air pressure in the bladder becomes too high the safety valve will pop off and release air until the bladder is at a safe pressure. The BC also has a bracket and straps to hold your tank.

A power inflator is attached to the BC with two hoses, a low-pressure hose and a high-pressure hose. There are two buttons on the power inflator that controls two valves, one from each hose. This is how you inflate and deflate your BC. The high-pressure hose comes from the first stage regulator, we'll cover the first stage regulator later. You push its button to add air to your BC. The low-pressure hose comes from your BC. You push its button to release air from your BC.

Most of your diving equipment floats so in order for you to go under water you need weights. There are several ways to add weights but usually divers use a weight belt or an integrated BC to carry most of the weights.

A weight belt is a belt with weights put in pockets or weights attached to it. Weight belts are popular but when you walk around, the weight is on your hips making it harder to walk. The integrated BC has pockets you put your weights in so you don't need a weight belt. You carry all the weight on your shoulders making it easier to walk. The integrated BC is also like a backpack with a balloon or bladder that will hold air and it also has a bracket and straps to hold your tank.

For additional weight you can also add ankle weights. These are small weights you can strap around your ankles. While going along underwater if your feet are floating up causing you to be uncomfortable. You can add ankle weights so you will be level and comfortable.

The tanks are made out of either aluminum or steel. Aluminum is less expensive but will be positive or float the lower it gets on air. Most steel tanks are negative or sink whether they're full or empty so with a steel tank you'll need to carry less weight than with an aluminum tank.

The tank has a valve on the top that you open by turning it to the left, just like taking a cap off a soda bottle, and close it by turning it to the right, or putting the cap on a soda bottle. On the valve there is also a burst disk. If the air pressure in the tank gets too high the burst disk will burst or rupture releasing all the air, saving the tank from rupturing. Two common ways to cause the air pressure to get too high in the tank are by overfilling it or leaving it in your car on a hot day with the windows up. The heat will cause the pressure to increase.

The first stage regulator is attached to the tank's valve. It's attached with a simple o-ring and screw type clamp. The tank can have up to three thousand pounds of air pressure in it. The first stage regulator regulates the air from the tank down to a hundred and fifty pounds of air pressure. The first stage regulator also has a bypass built into it. This bypassed air is air directly from the tank for the pressure gauge so you can tell how much air pressure is in your tank.

The second stage regulator is the regulator you put in your mouth and breath with. It has a hose that is attached to the first stage regulator. The second stage regulator regulates the hundred and fifty pounds of air pressure from the first stage regulator down to breathable air. The second stage regulator also has an exhaust valve you exhale through. When you breathe in using the mouthpiece you get breathable air and when you breathe out or exhale the exhaust valve opens automatically releasing your exhaled air. All you do is breathe in and breathe out just like being above water and just about that easy too.

It is recommended that you have an alternate air source, usually they are called an octopus or backup regulator. An alternate air source is just an extra second stage regulator in case something happens to your second stage regulator, you'll be able to switch regulators and breathe or if your dive buddy runs out of air they can use your alternate air source to breath with. The alternate air source has its own hose that comes from your first stage regulator, just like your second stage regulator has. Some power inflators have a second stage regulator built into them, with this type of power inflator one hose from the first stage regulator is all that's needed. That way you'll have one less hose to deal with or to get tangled up on something.

During your dive training you will be using a depth gauge and a timing device and diving with the dive charts. After the dive training most divers use a dive computer instead of using the dive charts. There are two main reasons for this, one reason is a dive computer is easy to use compared to the charts and the other reason is you can stay down longer with a computer. We'll explain more in part four of the training videos.

The pressure gauge is exactly as it sounds. It reads how much air pressure is in the tank. It has a hose that is attached to the bypass on the first stage regulator. Most pressure gauges will have a red area around five hundred pounds to let you know you're getting dangerously low on air.

The depth gauge is exactly as it sounds. It reads the depth that you're at. Most depth gauges also have a moveable hand. You move the moveable hand to read on the zero depth before you go diving. As you descend down, the depth gauge will read your depth. The depth gauge hand will also push the moveable hand along with it as long as you're going deeper. When you start ascending up the moveable hand won't move and stay at the deepest depth you went. After the dive you will need to know the deepest depth you went for the dive charts.

When most people dive they go straight out, turn around and come straight back in. These are easy dives to navigate. Most diving compasses have a heading marker and an opposite heading marker that is at one hundred and eighty degrees. So you just set your heading going out and when you're ready to come back, stay on the opposite heading marker to come straight back in.

A console is a holder to hold the pressure gauge, depth gauge and compass. The gauges are mounted in a console so they are all protected, neat and close together for your convenience.

The timing device or watch must be waterproof and should have a movable minute dial around the outside of the face of the watch. This moveable minute dial is for you to set then be able to easily see how long you've been down. You turn the moveable minute dial pointer until it's pointing at the minute hand on your watch. Example if its 10:18 you point the moveable minute dial at the minute hand that's on the eighteen. When you come up you look at your watch and see what number your minute hand is pointing to on the dial. If the minute hand is pointing to thirty-two on your moveable minute dial. You've been underwater for thirty-two minutes. If you are diving with dive charts you will need to know how many minutes you were underwater.

The whistle is usually attached to the BC. The whistle is a safety signaling device only and not a toy. It should only be used in an emergency, not to signal your buddy that this looks like a good spot to go down. Do not ever play with your whistle.

Your dive light is a flashlight that's waterproof and can withhold pressure as you dive. It's a good idea to carry a small dive light even in the daytime. You never know when there'll be some dark place under a big rock or in a hole that you'll want to look into. At night you should carry two dive lights, your main one and a backup just in case your main one goes out. You don't want to be stuck at night underwater in the dark without a dive light.

You should have a dive knife not so much for protection from the animals but for cutting yourself out of kelp or fishing lines. It's usually not needed very often but when you do need one, it's nice to have it.

We hope you enjoyed this video and remember to always be aware and be safe.

I thought at least this movie was interesting but it sure did seem educational. I can't wait until we go diving. Ron walked in and turned the lights back up.

Ron said, "Any questions?" I said, "What about sharks." Ron started laughing and said, "That's always one of the first questions. *You're privileged to see a dangerous shark.* It's very rare to see one. You do see small docile sharks often but the biggest ones you'll usually see are only about three or four feet, if you're lucky. You probably should be more scared of barracuda than sharks. You're probably even more likely to be hit by lightening than to see a dangerous shark." Debbie quickly raised her hand and said, "I've been hit by lightening. I was standing next to a tree that lightening struck and it ended up hitting me too." Deb said, "Really. You did?" Debbie said, "Yeah but it didn't hit me directly so I wasn't hurt too bad." Deb said, "Man, that must have been scary." Debbie said, "Yeah it was."

Ron said, "Let's take a break and help yourselves to a soda if there is any in there" he started pointing at the little refrigerator in the corner of the room and said, "They're all donations. We just ask that you replace whatever you drink." We all said okay, walked over, got a soda, sat back down and started talking.

Ron walked out. We could hear him doing something, then he walked back in. He was holding a bunch of dive parts all held together with hoses. Ron said, "You guys ready." We all said, "Yes." Ron sat down and pointed to one of the parts that was about half as big as a soda can with a screw type clamp and had some hoses connected to it. Ron said, "This is the first stage regulator. It attaches with this clamp to the valve on your tank. It regulates the air from the tank down to a hundred and fifty pounds of pressure." Ron followed one of the hoses with his hand from the first stage regulator and said, "This is the second stage regulator it regulates the air pressure down to breathable air." He started pointing at the mouthpiece and said, "See the mouthpiece." We started shaking our heads yes. Ron said, "You see how it's attached. Only with these wire ties, and usually just two. There was a lady that almost drowned because her mouthpiece came off her second stage regulator. If something happens don't panic. She got a gulp of water, panicked and it almost cost her, her life. She was very lucky."

Ron unscrewed the big cap that is on the front of the second stage regulator. He took a round rubber part out and showed it to us. He then said, "This diaphragm can also crack and give you a mouth full of water. Always be aware and never panic." Ron started moving a little lever that is in the second stage regulator behind where the diaphragm was and said, "This little lever is what opens the air valve to give you breathable air."

Ron passed everything around to us to look at. We all took a good look at everything and passed it back to Ron. Ron put the second stage regulator back together and said, "Any questions so far?" I jokingly said, "I'm not going to be the one to use that regulator am I?" Everyone started laughing.

Ron was holding the first stage regulator in his left hand and followed a different hose to the gauges and said, "This is the console. It holds your pressure gauge, depth gauge and compass. The pressure gauge shows how much air is in your tank. The depth gauge shows how deep you are and this is your compass. Do you want to see a trick?" Ron got up, turned the lights off and shined a dive light onto the gauges, then turned off the dive light. All the gauges are lit up - they have that glowing stuff they put in some watches. Ron said, "If it's at night and your going up, just shine your dive light on the gauges for a few seconds to light them up. That way you won't have to hold your dive light on them to see them."

Ron turned the lights back on and followed a different hose down to a quick connect coupling on the end of it and said, "Does anyone know what this is used for?" He was clicking it over and over, like it was a hint. We all said, "No." Ron said, "It's for your power inflator. Since your power inflator is always attached to your BC with a low pressure hose, you have to hook up your high pressure hose to your power inflator with this quick connector. All of our power inflators have the alternate air sources or backup regulators built into them."

Ron started looking at some of his notes then asked, "Any questions?" We all said "No." Ron said, "Okay that's it for today's lessons. Try to read as much of the book that you can. It would be best if you read it all. You'll need to bring two small photos about the size of a passport photo with you on Thursday. You can get them at those photo booths if you want. There's one at the miniature golf place right down the street. One picture will be for your dive card and the other one is for our records."

We all stood up and started walking toward the front of the dive shop. It was dark and quiet. Everyone had gone home and the dive shop was closed. Ron said, "It's easier for me if you park in the back. That way I don't have to unlock the front door. The back door is usually unlocked and open to help cool down the classroom. If we all park in the back we all just walk out together." We all said okay and walked out.

We got in the car and started driving to Deb's house. I said, "Boy I'm worn out now. It's been a long time since I studied that hard. You're probably used to studying since you've been taking college classes." Deb said, "I'm a little tired but it was interesting. We need to get our pictures tomorrow." I said, "Okay. I'll come pick you up and we'll go get them." Deb said, "Okay."

We drove up to Deb's house. She got out and walked in. I drove home.

Wednesday …

I called Deb and asked, "You ready to go get your picture taken?" Deb said, "Yeah come pick me up." I drove over to Deb's and picked her up. We went to the miniature golf place and got our pictures then I took Deb home and I went home.

Thursday …

I called Deb and asked, "You ready?" Deb said, "Yeah come pick me up." I said, "Okay I'm on my way." I drove over to Deb's house and picked her up then drove to the dive shop and parked in the back. The parking lot was a little crowded with divers. They were carrying their tanks into the dive shop or carrying them out to their cars. We could hear the air compressor running constantly.

We walked in the back door. Eddie was filling the tanks. He was joking around and laughing. We walked to the classroom and sat down. Debbie walked in, sat down and then Ron walked in and said, "Let's get started." Ron walked over to the TV and VCR and turned them on, walked over and dimmed the lights. The video started …

This video is part two of four of the training videos. We hope you enjoy the video. We'll start with how to pack; how to put your dive gear together and put it on; how to get in the water and descend down; how to ascend up and get out of the water; and put up your dive gear.

You should always try to pack taking up as little space as possible. If you and your buddy drive to the beach in your van you'll have plenty of space to put your dive gear. But if you go with your buddy in his small car you'll need to pack carefully. Also if you go on a boat dive trip you could have twenty or thirty other divers in a small area. So plan your packing.

If you want you can buy a dive bag to put all your dive gear in. That way your fins aren't over there and your mask over here. They will all be in one neatly packed dive bag. Most of the time your weights and tank will be separate from your dive bag because of the weight. You would have a hard time carrying everything at once in your dive bag.

Once you're packed and arrive at your dive sight. You have to unpack and put it all together. First you should put your dive gear together. Then put your wetsuit on. If you put your wetsuit on first you'll get too hot and overheat. So put your wetsuit on last and at the same time your dive buddy starts putting their wetsuit on. So they won't have to wait and overheat waiting for you.

To start putting your dive gear together you'll need to stand your tank up on a flat surface then slide your BC over it and strap your tank straps around your tank. Check to make sure the straps are tight so your tank won't slide out of your BC. Tighten the clamp on the first stage regulator onto the valve on your tank and take your short air hose with the quick connect coupling and connect it to your power inflator. Open the air valve on your tank. If your BC is an integrated BC put your weights in their pockets. Now lay your BC, tank and regulators over so they can't be knocked over or fall over by accident. Your dive gear is now ready.

You're now ready to put your wetsuit on when your dive buddy is ready to put theirs on. After you have your wetsuit on put your weight belt on unless you have an integrated BC. Now your ready to put your tank, BC and regulators on or to simplify it your dive gear.

There are several ways to put your dive gear on. One way is to have your dive buddy pick up your dive gear then you just walk over and put your arms into the BC's shoulder straps. Then tighten your cummerbund that's the strap that goes around your stomach and your shoulder straps. Then you do the same for your dive buddy.

Now that you and your dive buddy have your dive gear on. You and your dive buddy needs to check each other. Is the air valve open? Are all the straps okay and not twisted? Does it sound like anything is leaking air. Just give each other a final check for anything that might not be put on right or doesn't look right.

Now get your mask, snorkel, fins and gloves and you're ready to head to the beach or if you're on a boat, your exit spot. When you're ready to make your entry make sure your air is on and your BC is inflated.

If you're doing a beach dive there are several different ways to get in. One of the popular ways is to get in the water, then put your fins on and kick out. You will float because your BC is inflated.

If you're doing a boat dive, walk up close to your exit spot. Put your fins and mask on and your regulator in your mouth. Walk up to the edge of the boat. Hold onto your mask and regulator with your hands. Then step off the boat. Because your BC is inflated you will float back to the surface after landing in the water.

If you know where you want to go down at you can kick to it on your back or snorkel to it. If kelp is between you and where you want to go down at it's usually easier to dive under the kelp canopy five feet or so and come back up on the other side than it is to snorkel through it. If your doing a boat dive most people go down the anchor line either by holding onto it or following it down.

Once you're at the spot where you're going down at put your mask on and your regulator in your mouth. Then slowly let the air out of your BC. As you start descending down equalize your ears before you feel pressure on them or they start hurting. You will need to equalize your ears several times as you descend down.

As you're descending down your dive gear and the air in your BC will be compressing from the pressure. So you will need to add air to your BC to keep you from descending too fast.

Once on the bottom you and your dive buddy should give each other the okay hand signal if everything is okay. As you're going along (normally just a foot or two off the bottom) you will need to control your buoyancy. If you notice you're using your hand to keep pushing off the bottom you'll need to add a little air to your BC. If you have to keep swimming down you'll need to dump air out of your BC. Controlling your buoyancy is like riding a bicycle eventually you'll get where you will stay where you want with little effort.

In case of an emergency, and only in an emergency, you can do an emergency ascent. You do this by dropping or dumping your weights either by unbuckling your weight belt and dropping it or by pulling the emergency straps on your integrated BC that will drop your weights. This is very dangerous and should only be done in an emergency.

After doing your dive and it's time to go up. You and your buddy should signal each other that it's time to go up by pointing up. If you did a boat dive it's a good idea to go back up the anchor line. Have your depth gauge or computer in your hand where you can see it clearly. Also have your power inflator in your hand to control your ascent. Ascending up your ears will equalize automatically so you won't have to worry about equalizing them.

Start swimming up. If your buoyancy is controlled it should be easy to start ascending up. Be ready to start dumping air out of your BC soon after you start ascending up. As you're going up your dive gear and the air in your BC will be expanding from being under less pressure. You want to go up at a rate of no more than forty feet per minute. Make sure you breathe normally while going up. Never hold your breath. Your lungs can be damaged if you hold your breath even for a short period.

Once on the surface air up your BC so you will float. Go ahead and take your regulator out of your mouth and your mask off or pull it down around your neck - that way you won't have to carry it.

Whenever you and your dive buddy are ready, go toward the beach but keep an eye on the surf. Usually the bigger waves come in sets that are a few minutes apart. So try to time going in when the waves are the smallest.

If you did a boat dive, go toward the back of the boat or to where the ladder is. Most dive boats have some type of platform on the back of the boat to make it easier to get out of the water.

After you finish your dives you'll need to start packing everything up. You'll need to disconnect all of your dive gear. If your BC is an integrated BC take your weights out of your BC to keep your dive gear from falling over. Shut the air valve on the tank. Disconnect the quick connect coupling from the first stage regulator to the power inflator. Disconnect your first stage regulator from your tank. Put your regulators and gauges in a safe place. Loosen the straps holding your tank onto your BC and slide your BC up off your tank. Now you need to pack everything.

Once you're at home, you need to rinse off and clean your dive gear right away. Don't wait until the next day. The ocean salt water is very hard on your dive gear. Some divers rinse everything off with a garden hose and some prefer soaking it in a barrel or drum. Either way is fine.

After everything is rinsed off hang it up or place it where it can dry. After it's dry you can put it up. You're now ready for your next dive trip.

We hope you enjoyed this video and remember to always be aware and be safe.

Ron walked in and turned the lights back up and said, "Lets take a break." We all said okay. Ron walked out of the classroom. We walked over, got a soda, sat back down and started talking.

After a few minutes Ron walked in, sat down and asked, "Any questions?" I said, "When do we pick up our dive gear?" Ron said, "You pick up your dive gear on Friday's, and bring it back clean on Monday's. The earlier you get down here the better off you are. The best equipment goes first. You'll only need to get one tank tomorrow. I just checked the surf forecast and they said the surf is small so we'll be diving at Corona Del Mar." Ron started handing us a paper then said, "Here's a map showing you how to get there. We'll meet there at 8:00 AM in the parking lot and don't forget any dive gear or you won't be diving. One of the papers we gave you has a list of dive gear you'll need. Check the list so you don't forget anything."

I asked, "How deep is it there?" Ron said, "Where we'll be it's around twenty feet. That's about all you need for dive lessons. What we'll do is meet at the parking lot every time. Then discuss what we'll be doing then go do it." Ron looked down and checked his paperwork then said, "Do you guys have any questions on anything so far?" We all said no. Ron said, "That's it for today then. Come down and get your dive gear tomorrow and we'll see you at the beach." We all said okay.

We all got up, walked to the back of the dive shop and out the back door. Ron locked the dive shop. We all walked to our cars, got in and drove out of the parking lot. Deb said, "This is going to be so much fun." I said, "I know. I can't wait." We drove up to Deb's house. She got out and walked in. I drove home.

Friday morning …

I called Deb and said, "You ready?" Deb said, "Yeah, come pick me up." I said, "Okay I'm on my way." I drove over to Deb's house and picked her up. Then we drove to the dive shop, parked in the back and walked in. Eddie was at a counter moving some dive gear around. I said, "Can we get some dive gear when you get a chance." Eddie said, "Sure. Just pick out a wetsuit and hood that you like" he started pointing over at some racks of wetsuits "then I'll get you your BC, regulators, weights and a tank."

Deb and I started looking at some wetsuits and hoods and tried some on. We found the ones we liked. We walked over to Eddie. Eddie handed us our BC's, weights and regulators then reached down and pulled out our tanks out of a rack under the counter.

We carried some of our dive gear to the car then went back in and got the rest of the dive gear. Deb and I thanked Eddie. Eddie said, "Your going to like it." Deb said, "I know it's going to be fun." We drove to Deb's house and she unloaded all her dive gear. I unloaded mine when I got home.

Saturday morning …

I loaded my dive gear in the car then called Deb and said, "You ready?" Deb said, "Yeah, come pick me up." I said, "Okay, I'm on my way." I drove over to Deb's house. She loaded her dive gear in the car.

We were on the way to Corona Del Mar. We stopped and got a couple of egg muffins for breakfast. We then drove to the parking lot, parked and started eating. We're a little early but Ron and some other divers are already here.

I thought this would be so much fun. I remembered back when Mom would bring us here when we were kids to look at the tidepools. They have all kinds of animals and creatures in them. We had so much fun back then. We even talked about wanting to be a scuba diver and see what was out in the ocean.

We finished eating. I looked over and saw a guy walking up to the car. I rolled the window down. He said, "Hello. I'm Ray. I'm training to be a dive instructor.

I'll be helping Ron out. So if you're ready go ahead and put your wetsuits on but don't worry about your dive gear. Just grab your mask and snorkel." Deb and I said, "Okay."

We put our wetsuits on and walked over to Ray's truck. Debbie was already there. Ray said, "Let's go do our first dive." We all started walking toward the water. Ray said, "All this dive is really for is to show you how your wetsuit makes you float and to practice with the mask and snorkel." We all said okay.

We walked to the water and started walking in. The water was chilly. We could feel the water seeping into our wetsuits. After a few minutes we were completely wet and warm. We were only chest-deep in the water. We all had six-millimeter one-piece wetsuits on. I was used to wearing a three-millimeter wetsuit because that's what I used for surfing. It would make me float a little bit but this one made me feel like a cork in the water. I could barely go under it made me float so much.

We all started clowning around. Ron swam out to us and said, "Okay we have some drills we have to do. First we need to just put our mask and snorkel on and practice breathing underwater with our snorkel." We all put them on and stuck our heads in the water. We kept breathing through our snorkels then Ron lifted his head out of the water. We lifted our heads out of the water. Ron said, "Now you need to put your head in the water using only your snorkel to breathe with no mask and without holding your nose. You'll think you will breathe in water but it's natural to breathe in and out of your mouth so, you'll be okay."

We all stood up. I put my snorkel in my mouth then slowly put my head in the water and concentrated on breathing. I slowly breathed in and slowly breathed out. I wasn't having any trouble breathing. I thought it was going to be harder. Ron lifted his head out of the water and so did we. Ron said, "This gives you a little practice to breathe without a mask so that if your mask comes off you can breathe until you get it back on. Now breathe through your snorkel while putting your mask on underwater and clear the water out of it by blowing air out of your nose. You all have drains in your mask so it'll be easy." I put my head in the water and concentrated on breathing through the snorkel. I slowly put my mask on. It's full of water. I slowly breathed in deeply then slowly blew the air out of my nose into the mask. I could see the water draining out. I slowly drained all the water out of my mask. I lifted my head out of the water and so did everyone else.

Ron said, "Let's get out and go put our dive gear on then meet back down here, but don't get into the water." We all said okay and started toward the beach. Deb and I got out of the water and walked to the car.

We unloaded our dive gear and started putting it together. I stood my tank up behind the car and slid my BC over it and tightened the tank straps. I got my regulators and clamped the first stage regulator onto the tank. I stepped back and looked at it. It looked funny. I said, "Deb do I have my first stage regulator on upside down?" Deb said, "I don't know but it doesn't look right." I kept looking at it and said, "I know. It doesn't." Ray walked up. I said, "Ray, do I have my first stage regulator on right?" He started looking at it, I could tell he wanted to laugh but he didn't. Ray said, "If your first stage regulator is on right then your second stage regulator will be on your right side. If it isn't then your first stage regulator is on upside down. You will need to turn yours over." Deb started laughing. I said, "I thought so! Thanks, Ray." I took it back apart and turned it around. Deb started putting hers together and said, "Here, watch how I put mine on."

We got our dive gear together. We opened our air valves and breathed in and out of our regulators, checking them. We put our weights into the pockets of our BC's. I picked my dive gear up, sat it on the car bumper then slipped my arms into the straps, stood up and tightened the straps. It was a little bit heavy but it wasn't too bad.

I walked over to help Deb pick hers up and put it on. We were excited. We grabbed our mask, snorkels and fins and started walking to the beach. Ray and Debbie were down there already. Deb and I walked over next to them. Ron and four other divers I've never seen before walked up. Ron said, "Okay. If everyone's air is turned on, air up your BC and pick a dive buddy. Then go ahead and get in the water and put your fins on."

I looked at the surf it was pretty small but it could still knock us down. We all aired up our BC's and got in the water, put our fins on, kicked out a little way and then formed a circle around Ron. Ron said, "Go ahead and put your mask on. You see that buoy out there." Ron started pointing to one of the buoy's that marks off the swimming area. "Put your regulator in your mouth, put your head in the water and kick out to that buoy."

Deb and I put our mask on, our regulators in our mouths, our heads in the water and started kicking toward the buoy. I was surprised at how easy it was to breathe using our regulators. Every now and then I looked up and made sure we were headed in the right direction. I couldn't believe it! Some of the other divers weren't watching where they were going. One was going to the right and another was turned around so much he was almost going back toward the beach.

We all finally made it to the buoy. Ron said, "I'm going to check your weight. This is the way I'm going to check it. Make sure your mask is on and your regulator is in your mouth. Then I'm going to hold your hand. Let all of your air out of your BC. If your weight is right the water level will be even with your eyes. When I squeeze your hand, air up your BC and come back up. Then I want you to grab hold of the buoy chain and slowly let the air out of your BC. Slowly go hand over hand down the buoy chain to the bottom. Do everything slow. It's about twenty feet deep here. When you get to the bottom get out of the way so the other divers can come down but stay together. Don't forget to equalize your ears they should never hurt. Stop and equalize them if you feel any pressure."

Ron called the other divers over that weren't in our class and started with them. He checked their weight then they went down. After they went down. Ron said, "They're already certified but they just wanted to do a few extra dives. You guys can do the same thing if you would like."

Ron said to Deb, "Come on over you can go first." Deb's eyes got really big. She went over to Ron and grabbed his hand. She put her regulator back in her mouth and let the air out of her BC. The water was even with her eyes. She came back up. Ron said, "Your weight is good. Go ahead and go down." Deb was ready to let her air out of her BC but she quickly took her regulator out of her mouth and said to Ron, "Okay if something goes wrong we shoot back up, right?" I almost started laughing but I held it back so I wouldn't scare her more. Ron looked at Deb and said in a real calm voice, "If there's a problem down there we fix it down there. You'll be fine just do everything slow." Deb said with a nervous voice, "Okay." Deb put her regulator back in her mouth and started going down.

Ron called me over. I was next. I started getting nervous. Ron grabbed my hand. I started letting the air out of my BC and started going down. The water level was even with my nose. Ron squeezed my hand. I aired up my BC and floated up. Ron said, "You could use a little more weight but you'll be okay. Grab the buoy chain and go ahead and go down."

I grabbed the buoy chain, let the air out of my BC and started going down feet first. It's an eerie feeling. I'm holding onto the chain and looking down. I can't see the bottom. Every few feet I can feel a little pressure on my ears so I stop and equalize them. It was a little tricky holding on to the buoy chain and using one finger on both of my hands to squeeze my nose all at the same time.

I was surprised at how easy it is to breathe under water. It's as easy as above water without a regulator. I can see everyone on the bottom. They're all looking up at me. I slowly kept going down. I got to the bottom and got on my hands and knees and crawled over next to Deb. We all stayed on our hands and knees waiting and looking at each other and looking up the chain.

The bottom is flat and sandy. We could only see for about ten feet. Debbie came down and crawled over next to Ray then Ron came down. Ron went up to everyone and gave us all the okay hand signal. We all gave it back to him. One at a time Ron signaled for each of the other divers to go back up the buoy chain. They all went up. Ron pointed at Deb to go back up the buoy chain. She crawled over to the chain and went up. Ron pointed at me to go up. I crawled over and grabbed the chain and started slowly going up hand over hand. I kept looking up.

I can see the buoy. I went up to the surface. Ray grabbed my arm and said, "Air up your BC, move out of the way and wait for Ron." I aired up my BC and kicked over next to Deb. I took my regulator out of my mouth. Debbie came up, then Ron. Ron said, "Okay that's all for today's diving. The first day is mainly to get the feeling of it. Let's get out and log our dive. Tomorrow we'll be doing two dives with our tanks and practicing exercises. You'll need to go down to the dive shop, have your tank aired up and pick up another tank. When you get home, clean your dive gear. Then get plenty of rest. We'll see you back down here in the morning."

Deb and I put our regulators back in our mouths and started kicking in. We were going slow and looking down into the water. We could barely see the bottom. Some divers went under us, on the bottom going out from the beach. We watched until they faded out of sight.

We can touch the bottom. We stood up, took off our fins, got out of the water then walked to the car and took our dive gear off. I said, "What do you think about keeping our wetsuits on and going swimming?" Deb said, "Okay." We loaded our dive gear in the car.

We walked back down to the water, went swimming and clowned around in the waves. Deb said, "I can't believe how warm the wetsuits keep you." I said, "I know I'm even a little hot." Deb said, "Me too." We swam around for awhile then got out.

We drove to the dive shop and carried our tanks in. Eddie was airing up tanks. He has a lot of them sitting at the filling area to air up. I said, "Is there any way you can fill these up too?" Eddie said, "Sure. I'll get them as soon as I can." I said, "Okay and when you get a chance we will need two more tanks. Ron said we'll need two tanks for our dives tomorrow." Eddie said, "Sure no problem. As soon as I start filling your tanks we'll go get them." Deb and I started talking to Eddie about diving while he was airing up the other tanks. Eddie started filling our tanks. We walked up to the front of the dive shop where the tanks are. Eddie said, "Just grab two you like and I'll mark it down that you checked them out." Deb and I started looking at the tanks. I grabbed one the same size I already had.

Deb grabbed a little one about the size of a gallon paint can and said, "I like this one." I started laughing. Eddie said, "That tank will probably be okay for you. Women get better air consumption than men." Deb said, "Good. I'll take it."

We walked back to the filling area. Eddie finished airing up our tanks. We loaded all the tanks into the car and started driving to Deb's house. I said, "I'll pick you up in the morning." Deb said, "Okay." We drove up to Deb's house. Deb unloaded her dive gear. I drove home, unloaded my dive gear and cleaned it.

Sunday morning …

I loaded my dive gear in the car. It's still wet. I called Deb and asked her if she was ready. Deb said, "Yeah, come get me." I said, "Okay I'm on my way." I drove over to Deb's house. She loaded her dive gear in the car.

We're on our way to Corona Del Mar. We stopped, got egg muffins then drove to the parking lot, parked and started eating. We're a little early again. We finished eating, sat in the car and talked.

Ray walked over and said, "We're about ready. You can put your dive gear together. Then meet at Ron's truck and he'll tell us when to put on our wetsuits." We said okay. Deb and I got out of the car, unloaded our dive gear and started putting it together. Deb said, "You think you can put your first stage regulator on right?" Then started laughing. I said, "I think I can but you better keep an eye on me."

We put our dive gear together then walked over to Ron's truck. Two of the other divers along with Ray and Debbie walked up right after us. Ron said, "Okay. What we're going to do is go out to the buoy. Then we'll check our weight. Then we'll go down the buoy chain. Once everyone is on the bottom we'll go along the bottom. Work on staying neutrally buoyant. Give your BC just little amounts of air so you won't have to keep pushing off the bottom. If you're floating up, let some air out of your BC. If everyone is ready let's go put our wetsuits and dive gear on and meet on the beach. Don't mess around or we'll overheat." Everyone said okay and walked back to their cars.

Deb and I started putting our wetsuits on. They're wet and cold. We kept going ewe-eee as we're putting them on. We got them on, opened up our air valves and checked our regulators. I put my dive gear on then helped Deb puts hers on.

We started walking to the beach. Ron was right. We were already getting hot. We all walked over next to Ron and started walking with him. Ron said, "Okay make sure your air is on, air up your BC then you and your dive buddy go ahead and get in. We'll meet at the buoy. Use your snorkels so you'll save your air."

Deb and I aired up our BC's, got in the water, put our fins on and snorkeled out to the buoy.

Ron called the other two divers over and checked their weight. They went down. Ron called Deb over and said, "Let's check your weight. Hold my hand and let your air of your BC." Deb let her air out of her BC. She went down to where the water was even with her eyes. Just like yesterday. She came back up. Ron said, "Your weight is good. Go ahead and go down the buoy chain." Deb let the air out of her BC and started going down.

Ron called me over and grabbed my hand and said, "Let's check your weight." I let the air out of my BC. The water level was even with my nose. Ron squeezed my hand. I went up. Ron said, "You're okay. Go ahead and go down." I grabbed the buoy chain and started letting the air out of my BC. I slowly started going down the buoy chain equalizing my ears along the way. I looked down at the bottom and could see everyone looking up watching me as I was coming down. I got to the bottom, went over next to Deb and started looking up the anchor chain.

Debbie started down. We watched her come down. She went next to Ray. Ron came down and gave everyone the okay hand signal. We all gave it back.

Ron pointed with his finger ahead like that is the direction he wants us to go. We all got side by side and started going along the bottom. Ron and Ray were staying about a foot or two off the bottom without any trouble. The rest of us were pushing off the bottom then floating up too much. We were working on our buoyancy but we weren't very good. Ron and Ray were going along really smooth - like pros. We kept going along practicing on our buoyancy - none of us new divers did it very well.

Ron started waving at everyone then started pointing at his pressure gauge. He gave each one of us the okay signal. We checked our air and gave him the okay signal back. We kept slowly going, working on our buoyancy. Ron waved at everyone and stopped.

Ron grabbed his power inflator and put it over his head. He was letting us know it's easier to let the air out of our BC's that way. Ron gave everyone the stop hand signal he didn't want us going up until he told us to. Ron pointed to Debbie. She put her power inflator up like Ron had his. She started kicking up toward the surface. Ron pointed at Deb. Deb started kicking up toward the surface. Ron pointed at me. I held my power inflator up and started kicking up. I let some air out of my BC on the way up but it wasn't much. I'm on the surface. Ray said, "Air up your BC and wait for Ron." The other divers came up one at a time and finally, Ron came up.

Ron said, "Let's get out and log our dive, change tanks and have our surface interval. Be sure to log your wetsuit, tank, weights and if you were positive or negative or just about right. That way you'll have a better idea of how much weight you need. I'll let you know when it's time for our next dive."

Deb and I put our regulators in our mouths and started kicking in. We're close enough to touch. We took our fins off and got out of the water. We walked to the car. We changed tanks and logged our dive. We started talking about how much fun it was and how easy it is to breathe under the water.

I started getting hot so I pulled the top part of my wetsuit down and so did Deb. We walked over to Ron's truck. Ron said, "What do you think so far?" Deb said, "It's really neat. I like it." We all started talking.

After a few minutes Ray, Debbie and the other two divers walked up. Ron said, "On our next dive, when I come up to you I'm going to give you the out of air signal and take my regulator out of my mouth. I want you to grab your alternate air source with your left hand. Then grab your regulator with your right hand. Take your regulator out of your mouth blowing little bubbles out the whole time until you put your alternate air source in your mouth. Then you hand me your regulator to breathe with. This is called buddy breathing. We'll give each other the okay signal and then I'll give you back your regulator. After everyone does it we'll go work on our buoyancy." We all started talking about buddy breathing and taking our regulators out of our mouths and then walked back to our cars.

After awhile, Ron started waving at everyone to come over to his truck. He said, "Okay. If everyone is ready let's put on our dive gear and meet on the beach. Any questions?" Everyone looked at each other and shook our heads no.

Deb and I walked back to the car and pulled our wetsuits back up. They were really cold now. We opened up our air, checked our regulators, put our dive gear on and started walking to the beach. We saw Ray and Debbie so we walked over to them, and with them to the beach.

We were looking at the small waves. I said, "They sure are small but they sure have good shape. If they were a little bigger they would be fun to surf." Ray said, "You're a surfer." I said, "Yeah, I've been surfing quite a while but I'm not that good." Ray said, "You're probably better than me getting in and out through the surf. If you help Deb, then I can help the other divers and not worry about you guys." I said, "Sure. We won't have any trouble getting in or out. Don't worry about us."

Ron and the other two divers walked up. Ron said, "Make sure your air is on, air up your BC, then you and your dive buddy get in the water and we'll meet at the buoy." Deb and I aired up our BC's, got in the water, put our fins on and snorkeled out to the buoy.

Ron said, "Does everyone have the same size tank that you had on the last dive?" Debbie and I along with the other two divers said yes. Deb said, "No. I have a smaller tank." Ron said, "We'll have to check your weight Deb but everyone else's weight will be okay. So we won't have to weight you." Ron said to the other two divers to go ahead and go down the buoy chain. He started pointing at Debbie and I and said, "but you two wait until I tell you to." Debbie and I both said okay. The other two divers went over to the buoy and went down.

Ron said to Deb, "Let's check your weight." Deb kicked over close to him and grabbed his hand and let the air out of her BC. The water was even with her mouth. Deb came back up. Ron said, "You'll be okay. Go ahead and go down the buoy chain." Deb grabbed the chain and started down.

Ron looked at me and said, "Go ahead." I grabbed the buoy chain and started letting the air out of my BC. I slowly started going down the buoy chain equalizing my ears on the way. I looked down at the bottom and could see everyone on their knees and looking up at me. I got to the bottom and went over next to Deb. Debbie started down. We watched her come down. She went over next to Ray. Ron came down. Ron gave everyone the okay hand signal. We all gave it back.

We all got in a circle around Ron. Ron went in front of Debbie and gave her the okay signal. She gave it back. Ron gave Debbie the out of air signal and took his regulator out of his mouth and dropped it to his side. He started pointed at his mouth. He turned and showed everyone little bubbles coming out of his mouth. He looked back at Debbie and pointed to her alternate air source. She grabbed her alternate air source and took her regulator out of her mouth and blew bubbles until she put her alternate air source in her mouth. She started breathing with her alternate air source and handed her regulator to Ron. Ron started using her regulator. Ron gave Debbie the okay signal. Debbie gave it back. Ron took her regulator out of his mouth and started using his own regulator. Debbie changed back to her regulator.

Ron came over in front of me. I grabbed my alternate air source and regulator. Ron gave the out of air signal and took his regulator out of his mouth and dropped it. I took my regulator out of my mouth. I started blowing little bubbles out of my mouth then put my alternate air source in my mouth and started breathing with it. I handed my regulator to Ron. Ron started using my regulator then gave me the okay signal. I gave it back. Ron took my regulator out of his mouth and started using his own regulator. I changed back to my regulator.

Ron went over in front of Deb. We watched her do the same thing. She didn't have any problems. Ron gave the other two divers the okay signal. They gave it back.

Ron pointed with his finger in the direction he wanted us to go. We all got side by side and started going along the bottom. Ron and Ray were going smoothly along the bottom but the rest of us were pushing off the bottom then floating up too much. We kept going and working on our buoyancy. We kept going along, practicing.

Ron started waving at everyone then started pointing at his pressure gauge. He gave each one of us the okay signal. We checked our air and gave him the okay signal back. We kept slowly going working on our buoyancy.

Ron waved at everyone and stopped. We all stopped. Ron pointed to Debbie and pointed up. Debbie put her power inflator over her head and started kicking up toward the surface. Ron pointed at Deb. Deb put her power inflator over her head and started kicking up toward the surface. Ron pointed at me. I put my power inflator over my head and started kicking up.

I'm on the surface. Ray said, "Air up your BC, move out of the way and wait for Ron." I aired up my BC and took my regulator out of my mouth. I said okay while kicking over next to Deb and Debbie. One of the other divers came up, then the other one, then Ron. Ron said, "We'll call it good for today's diving. Let's get out, put up our dive gear and log our dive. Be sure you clean your dive gear when you get home and take it back to the dive shop tomorrow." Ron started pointing at Deb, Debbie and I and said, "I'll see you three at the dive shop Tuesday for our next lesson." Deb, Debbie and I said okay. Ron said, "Everyone did a great job." We all put our regulators back in our mouths and started kicking in.

We're close enough to touch. We took our fins off, got out of the water and walked to the car. Deb said, "Man am I worn out." I said, "Me too but it sure was fun." We took off our dive gear and packed it in the car.

We're on our way home. I said, "Do you want me to pick you up tomorrow to take your dive gear back?" Deb said, "Yeah. Call me when you're ready." I said, "Okay." We drove up to Deb's house. She unloaded her dive gear. I went home, unloaded my dive gear and cleaned it.

Monday …

I called Deb and said, "You ready?" Deb said, "I'm ready." I said, "I'm on my way." I loaded my dive gear then drove to Deb's house. Deb loaded her dive gear.

We drove to the dive shop and parked in the back. There were racks full of wet dive gear outside the back door. Deb and I carried our tanks in and put them at the filling area. Eddie said, "You can hang your wetsuits and BC's up on the racks outside. Put your weights with the other weights outside and bring me your regulators." Deb and I said okay and went back out to the car, unloaded everything, put it with the other dive gear, then carried our regulators in and handed them to Eddie. Eddie was busy working with dive gear. I said, "Thanks Eddie, we'll see you tomorrow." Eddie said, "Okay" and kept working. Deb and I walked back out to the car. I drove Deb home then I went home.

Tuesday …

I called Deb and said, "You ready for number three?" Deb said, "Yeah, come pick me up." I said, "Okay I'm on my way." I drove over to Deb's house and picked her up then drove to the dive shop and parked in the back.

We walked in the back door and up to the front of the dive shop. Eddie was talking to a lady next to the counter. Eddie waved at us. We waved back. Deb and I started looking around at the wetsuits. Deb said, "I like this one but I don't think it'll fit me." I said, "I like this one." Eddie walked over to us and said, "You can try them on over there." He started pointing at a little door at the side of the dive shop and said that we could change in the change room if we wanted to. Deb and I looked at where he was pointing and said, "Okay."

Deb said to Eddie, "Do you think this wetsuit will fit me?" Eddie said, "We don't have that many women's wetsuits but some women wear men's wetsuits." I started laughing really hard. Deb and I looked at each other. Deb didn't seem to think it was as funny as I did. Eddie said, "Go ahead and try these on and if none of them fit, try to figure out what size you need. Then we'll order it" Deb said, "Oh okay, I like this one hopefully it'll fit." Eddie said, "If you gain weight or don't like the way it fits I know a tailor that can modify your wetsuit for you. He's been working on mine a lot lately." Eddie starting laughing and patting his stomach.

The lady Eddie was talking to before walked over to us. Eddie said, "This is Kate. She's your dive instructor tonight." Deb said, "You're a dive instructor?" Kate said, "Yeah, I'm training to be one - actually what I want to do is be a dive instructor on cruise ships." Deb said, "Oh, that sounds like fun." Debbie walked up from the back of the dive shop. Kate said, "Yeah, I think so too."

Kate said, "It's about time to start the class." She started walking toward the classroom. We all walked with her. Kate said to Debbie, "I'll be your instructor tonight." Debbie said, "Okay." Kate walked over to the TV and VCR and turned them on. She then walked over and dimmed the lights, sat down and started watching the video with us. The video started …

This video is part three of four of the training videos. We hope you enjoy the video. We'll be going over the things that will be happening to you underwater while your diving. Let's go ahead and get started.

Water causes objects to appear out of focus. The air in your mask will allow your eyes to focus. Your mask will cause objects to be twenty five percent closer and thirty three percent larger to you. The water absorbs light, which affects the colors you see underwater so when you go deeper than sixty feet about the only colors you see are different shades of gray. So the more colorful dives are less than sixty feet. However shining your dive light on objects will restore their color.

Humans communicate usually by hearing and speaking. Both of these are affected underwater. Sound travels four times faster in water than in air. On land, sound is so slow that your closest ear to the sound hears it and then the other ear hears it causing you to determine which direction it came from. In water, sound is so fast that it seems both ears hear it at the same time causing you not to be able to tell what direction it came from. You can hear a boat motor very clear but you can't tell which direction it's headed. Speaking or yelling can be done but it's very hard to do and not very clear. Most divers communicate with a slate and pencil or by using hand signals.

You should never run out of air but if you do, or if your regulators fail, you and your buddy will be air sharing. You should go to your buddy and give them the out of air hand signal. Your buddy should then start using their alternate air source or backup regulator and give you their regulator to breath with. After both divers are comfortable they should start their controlled ascent holding on to each other to keep from getting separated.

The air pressure around us is 14.7 pounds of pressure or one bar. For every thirty three feet of water you go down it's another 14.7 pounds of pressure or one more bar. So when you're at the depth of thirty three feet you're under 29.4 pounds of pressure or two bars. Sixty six feet is 44.1 pounds of pressure or three bars. Ninety nine feet is 58.8 pounds of pressure or four bars and a hundred and thirty two feet is 73.5 pounds of pressure or five bars.

Since air is compressible, if you go down to thirty three feet and take one breath of air it's the same volume as one breath on the surface. If you blew all that air into a balloon then went up to the surface and took the balloon with you it would be twice as big or twice as much volume. If you breathed one breath in the balloon at sixty six feet, when you got to the surface it would be three times as big or three times the volume and so on. So the deeper you go the faster you'll use up your air and the faster you'll breath in high amounts of nitrogen.

Air is about twenty percent oxygen and eighty percent nitrogen. Decompression sickness or "the Bends" is caused by increased nitrogen breathed in by the lungs. That breath of air you breathed in at thirty three feet is under twice the pressure that you breathe in on the surface making it twice as much nitrogen and oxygen. At sixty six feet it's three times as much nitrogen and oxygen and so on. So as you go down or descend, the nitrogen amount increases and your body absorbs the nitrogen and keeps it in solution. When you go back up toward the surface the pressure decreases and your body releases the nitrogen. It is important that you come up slow enough to allow the nitrogen to stay in solution. If you go up too fast, the nitrogen comes out of solution and forms gas bubbles creating decompression sickness.

A good example of this is like a bottle of soda that has been shaken. It is soda and a little space of air at the top. The soda is in solution. When you twist the cap slightly, the soda turns foamy. The soda is then out of solution.

The main way to prevent decompression sickness is to return to the surface slow enough so the nitrogen can release from your body without coming out of solution. A safe way to do this is to go up slower than forty feet a minute and stopping at fifteen feet for five minutes for a safety stop before going to the surface.

You should never hold your breath. If you fail to keep your airway open to your lungs while you go up, it could cause you to have an air embolism. Trapped air in the lungs will expand and could cause tissue ruptures and air bubbles to pass into the blood stream. The blood then carries these air bubbles into smaller arteries until a blockage forms and restricts blood flow. Symptoms can be anywhere from slight numbness to death.

The human body is about seventy percent water and about thirty percent solids and also gases. The water and solids aren't compressible but the gases are. The gases are in the air spaces of the sinuses, lungs and middle ears. Your sinuses and lungs will equalize as you breath but you'll need to equalize your ears by holding your nose and blowing until you feel them equalize.

Although diving is a safe activity, you should try to stay in good shape by eating good, regular exercise and get regular medical check ups - especially if you smoke, are overweight, on medication or have medical problems that might be of concern. If you are not familiar with first aid and CPR it is recommended that you take them. Not only for your diving experiences but also for the safety of the ones around you.

Nitrogen narcosis is a narcotic effect on divers caused by high pressure nitrogen. It may or may not happen to you but if it does, it usually gets worse the deeper you go. The depth it can happen has not been determined but most divers have had it happen in the eighty to hundred feet range. Nitrogen narcosis is one of the main reasons it is recommended that divers stay less than a hundred feet. However, with proper training, deeper dives can be made safely. Nitrogen narcosis can cause you to act and feel mentally abnormal. It is not known why nitrogen causes this. We hope you have enjoyed this video and remember to always be aware and be safe.

Kate walked over and turned the lights back up. Ron came in and sat down with us. Kate said, "Do you guys want to take a break and stretch your legs?" We all said yes. I said to Ron, "I'm going to buy my own dive gear. Is there any way you could help me pick it out? I don't know anything about what I'm doing." Ron said, "Sure. Why don't you come down to the dive shop tomorrow and we'll look at it." I said, "Okay. Thanks Ron."

After awhile we all sat back down. Kate started teaching to us. She was more or less reading out of her instructor's manual. We could tell she was training to be an instructor. Ron is a good instructor for her and a good teacher for us. Ron knew all the answers and how to explain everything really well. When Kate started getting stuck, Ron would just say a few words then everything would fit into place and seem so reasonable. Kate said, "You should always do your deepest dive first" then she looked at Ron like she wanted to tell us something. Ron looked at us and said, "That is very important. You should always do your deepest dive first, and you should stop at fifteen feet for five minutes unless you're doing a beach dive. If you're doing a beach dive you're slowly coming back up to the surface so it's not necessary. You should never come back with less then five hundred pounds of air."

Kate kept teaching then asked if we had any questions. I said, "Nitrogen Narcosis is weird." Kate said, "Yes it is and usually all you have to do is go up and it usually stops." Ron said, "Just a few feet is all you have to go up - not all the way to the surface." I said, "That's really strange. Did I hear that right that the deeper you go the faster you use up your air?" Kate said, "Yes. After just a few minutes when you're deep, you'll use up all of your air. As a matter of fact, we have a guy here at the dive shop that ran out at around a hundred feet. They said he was going up to other divers while he was on his way to the surface but he never made contact with them, because he felt he needed to get to the surface." Kate started to smile and looked over at Ron then she started talking about the video. Kate said, "Any questions?" We all shook our heads no.

Kate said, "Okay that's it for today's lesson. We'll see you back here Thursday." We all said okay.

We all got up, walked to the back of the dive shop and out the back door. Ron locked the dive shop. We walked to our cars, got in and drove out of the parking lot. We drove up to Deb's house. I said, "I'll pick you up Thursday." Deb said, "Okay." I drove home.

Wednesday …

I drove to the dive shop and parked in the back. I walked in the back door and up to the front of the dive shop. Eddie was working behind the counter. I asked if Ron was around because he said he would help me to pick out some dive gear. Eddie said, "Yes he is. I'll go get him." Eddie walked over to Ron's office. Ron walked out from his office with some catalogs and said, "Are you ready to pick out some dive gear?" I said, "Yeah." Ron said, "We'll pick it out and then they should deliver it either Thursday or Friday." I said, "Okay." Ron put the catalogs down on the counter. I said, "I would like dive gear that works really good but it doesn't have to look real fancy or anything. Just function well." Ron said, "Are you planning on doing underwater work?" I said, "Yeah, I'm planning on helping people raise their boats after they've been sunk and stuff like that." Ron said, "You'll want good balanced regulators then so you won't have trouble breathing when your doing heavy work." Ron opened up one of the catalogs and pointed at a regulator. He said, "I would recommend this first stage regulator" then he turned some pages and said, "and this second stage regulator." I said, "Okay."

Ron said, "What about your BC? I would recommend an integrated BC. They're easier to carry then a BC and weight belt. Are you planning on doing heavy lifting with it? The reason I ask is because this BC (he started pointing at a BC in the catalog) can lift a lot but it also has a lot of drag when you're moving. So if you're going to be doing a lot of moving you'll get tired easy. But this one (he started pointing to a different BC in the catalog) doesn't have much drag but it can still lift quiet a bit - just not as much as the other one." I said, "I'm planning on lifting anchors and stuff like that but I'm going to be moving around a lot too." Ron said, "The second one would probably be best for you then." I said, "Okay."

Ron picked up a different catalog and opened it and said, "I use this power inflator. It has a second stage regulator built into it. I really like it. With it you don't have a separate hose for your octopus since your power inflator and backup regulator are together." I said, "I'll take it."

Ron said, "I would recommend a computer. Computers are all about the same except some have more memory to keep track of more dives and some have a built in pressure gauge. You can spend a little or you can spend a lot." I said, "I just want the basic computer then. I'll be logging all my dives so I won't need the computer to keep them in memory." Ron said, "This computer" while pointing at a computer in the catalog "is the best computer for the money. It keeps your last five dives in memory. If you buy this computer I'll throw in a console with a compass and a pressure gauge for free." I said, "Sounds good to me. I'll take it." Ron said, "The computer will take about a week and a half to get. The console will come with a depth gauge in it. When you get the computer just take the depth gauge out of the console and put in the computer." I said, "Okay."

Ron said, "I use a steel tank. That way I don't have to carry so much weight." I said, "My brother has an aluminum eighty so I think I want the same. That way, we'll both have the same tanks. As a matter of fact, can I get two tanks? That way I can do two dives." Ron said, "Sure it takes about two weeks to get the tanks but if you need tanks we'll loan them to you until you get yours." I said, "Good, thanks." Ron said, "What color do you want them?" I said, "Blue. That's my favorite color."

Ron said, "What about your wetsuit?" I said, "I was looking at the one's on the racks but I wasn't sure about them." Ron said, "I use a six millimeter farmer John with a four millimeter hooded vest. That works well for me. I hardly ever get cold." I said, "That's what I want then. I saw one I liked on the rack that was a six millimeter farmer John." Ron and I walked over to the wetsuit rack. I pointed at the one I liked and said, "This one." Ron said, "Yeah that's a good one" then he pointed at a different rack and said, "and if you want a good hooded vest these are good." I said okay and grabbed one that looked like it would fit.

Ron said, "You'll probably need about twenty four pounds of weights" and pointed to some weights in a shelf. I told Ron okay and picked out twenty four pounds.

We walked back to the counter. I put the weights down. Ron started adding everything up. I walked to the change room, tried on the wetsuit and hooded vest. They fit perfect. I walked back over to the counter, put the wetsuit and hooded vest down. I noticed some gloves. I tried on a pair and put them on the counter. Ron said, "Do you want to make payments?" I said, "No I think I have enough to pay for it. Will you take a check?" Ron said, "Sure. We'll give you a call as it comes in." I said, "Okay, thanks Ron." I carried everything out to the car and drove home and unloaded my new equipment.

I drove to the warehouse store and started looking at their waterproof watches. I found one I really liked and bought it then drove back home.

I called my brother, David. He moved in with mom to help her. He's already a certified diver and has all of his dive gear. I said, "I bought my dive gear today and I bought two tanks in case we want to do two dives. That way I won't have to rent one." David said, "That's a good idea. Can you get me another tank? I've only got one." I said, "Sure what color do you want? I got both of mine blue." David said, "I want different colors that way it will be easy to tell them apart. I might just always use one color first. That way I won't get a full tank mixed up with an empty one." I said, "I should have gotten different colors too but I wasn't thinking about that when I ordered them." David said, "I've got a yellow one so any color but yellow or blue. Try to get white if you can and if they don't have that just get any color." I said, "Okay but I'm sure I can get white. If everything goes right we'll be finished with the dive training on Sunday." David said, "Good I'm ready to go diving." I said, "Me too - it's going to be fun."

Thursday …

I called Deb and said, "You ready for the last class?" Deb said, "Yeah, come pick me up." I said, "Okay. I'm on my way." I drove to Deb's house and picked her up. Deb said, "Scott wants to go with us this weekend. He said he'll take the truck and drive if you want." I said, "Okay sounds good to me. Call me when you guys are on the way and I'll be ready." Deb said, "Okay."

We drove up to the dive shop, parked in the back and walked in. Ron was behind the counter. I walked over to Ron and said, "My brother wants me to order him an aluminum eighty." Ron said, "No problem. What color does he want?" I said, "Do you have white?" Ron said, "That shouldn't be any problem. I'll try and get it in with yours." I said, "Okay, thanks Ron." I looked down at my watch and said, "What do you think about my new dive watch?" Ron said, "That's a nice one." I said, "It's only good for a hundred meters though." Ron said, "How deep are you planning on going?" I said, "I read in a magazine you should buy dive watches rated for at least a hundred and fifty meters because they're more heavy duty." Ron said, "That one is plenty heavy duty." I said, "I thought it looked like it was."

Debbie walked in. Ron said, "You guys ready to start?" We all said yes. I said, "Where's Kate?" Ron said, "She took tonight off." We all walked to the classroom and sat down. Ron walked over to the TV and VCR and turned them on, then walked over and dimmed the lights. The video started …

This video is part four of four of the training videos. We hope you enjoy the video. Let's get started with the dive tables. The navy developed dive tables to keep divers from taking in too much nitrogen into their body's and then having to do a decompression stop before surfacing. As you look at the tables the depth is the deepest point you went even if it was for a brief time. The bottom time is the time you were underwater.

To figure the dive tables after your dive you take the deepest depth you went and the length of time you were down. On the top section of the dive table go down the depth column and find your depth then go across to the right and find your bottom time. Straight up from your bottom time will be a letter A, B, C up to K. This is your group letter. Now go to the middle section of the dive table. Locate your group letter on the diagonal letters. Go to the right and find your surface interval, your surface interval is how long you have been on the surface since you came up from your dive. Now go down from that time to the bottom section to your new group letter. Now determine the depth you're planning on going on your next dive. Look for that depth to the left in the repetitive dive depth column. Go to the right to your group letter. This will give you your residual nitrogen time in minutes; this is the nitrogen you have already in your body from your first dive.

Go back to the top section and find the depth you're planning on going on your next dive. Next to that depth is the maximum minutes you can be at that depth. Now subtract your residual nitrogen minutes from your maximum minutes. This now leaves you with your length of time you can be at your planned depth on your next dive.

Most divers don't like or use dive tables because you cannot stay down very long with them. The reason is because you have to use the deepest depth you went for the entire time you did your dive.

Most divers use dive computers. Dive computers account for the length of time you were at each depth. So if you go to seventy feet for five minutes then up to thirty feet for fifteen minutes. Using the dive tables you would have to use seventy feet for the entire twenty minute dive. Dive computers will calculate seventy feet for five minutes then thirty feet for fifteen minutes letting you have a lot longer dive. Then once you're on the surface your dive computer will keep track of your surface time and have a readout for planning your next dive showing you how long you can be at each depth.

It's a good idea to log your dives. Logging your dives is a good way of keeping notes on your equipment, like need more weight and so on. It's also nice to refer back to previous and memorable dives.

You should check on the conditions of your dive location before going diving, like surf and tides. If the surf is high it might be a good idea to find a more protected dive location. High surf can also cause heavy surge, which can be dangerous. If the tide is low some locations are hard to get in and out of because of rocks and hazards.

There are many types of underwater life you will see, marine plants, marine animals and fish. Some can be dangerous such as barracuda, sharks, even the plant life can be dangerous like getting tangled up in kelp. It's a completely different world down there waiting for you to see and visit so let's go diving. We hope you enjoyed this video and remember to always be aware and be safe.

Ron walked in, turned the lights back up and said, "Why don't we take a break." We all said okay, got up and started moving around.

After awhile we all sat back down. Ron said, "After you get certified if you want to you can sign up for specialty classes. We usually do one each week. If you pay for two we'll give you three. We have deep diving, boat diving, night diving, wreck diving, navigating and photography." I said, "What is deep diving?" Ron said, "Certified diving is up to a hundred feet. Certified deep diving is up to a hundred and thirty feet." I said, "Where do you do the deep diving at?" Ron said, "Redondo Pier usually. Sometimes we do the dive training there too, if the surf is up at Corona Del Mar." I said, "I know I want to do the deep diving." Ron said, "The specialty classes are easy and fun. You just read the book then come down and watch a movie. Then we'll do a dive with you. There's no testing. We're going to Catalina in a couple of weeks. We'll be doing a boat dive and a deep dive there and the next week will be a night dive."

I said, "I want to do deep diving, boat diving and night diving. I think I want to do them all." Ron said, "Also for the next year each month you'll get a dive magazine. They're free from the dive shop. Any questions before we do our test?" I said, "Yeah, give us some answers." Ron said, "I don't think you'll have much trouble."

Ron passed a test to each one of us. I started looking at the pages to see how long it was. It wasn't too bad, just three pages. I started working on it.

After a couple of minutes I could hear Deb and Debbie flip their page. I thought already, how could they be done with the first page already? Everyone kept working on their test.

Deb finished hers then Debbie. I kept working on mine. I could tell they were all looking at me and watching me. Finally I was finished.

Ron said, "Okay grade your own" then he started telling us the answers. I missed one then two. I thought oh my gosh. I'm the only one missing any then finally Debbie missed one. We were finally finished grading them. I missed two, Debbie missed one and Deb got a hundred.

Deb leaned toward me and said, "Uh hum one of us got a hundred." I said, "Yeah but mine was harder." Deb said, "I can't believe you missed two. You came in last place. I hope you're better at diving than you are at taking the test." I said, "You just got lucky."

Ron said, "Everyone passed. You're all done with the classroom work. Now you need to pick up your dive gear tomorrow and meet us at Corona Del Mar Saturday morning." We all said okay, got up, walked to the back of the dive shop and out the back door. Ron locked the dive shop. We walked to our cars, got in and drove out of the parking lot. We drove up to Deb's house. She got out and walked in. I drove home.

Friday ...

I called Deb and asked, "You ready?" Deb said, "Pick me up." I said, "Okay." I drove over to Deb's house, picked her up then drove to the dive shop, parked in the back and walked in. Eddie was filling a tank and looked up at me and said, "I just called your house and left you a message. Your dive gear just came in." I said, "Oh good."

We walked to the front of the dive shop. Eddie walked behind the counter and started picking up stuff from under the counter and putting it on top of the counter. Eddie said, "Here you go. Here's your BC, first stage regulator, second stage regulator, power inflator with your back up regulator built into it, your console with your compass, pressure gauge and depth gauge. When your computer comes in just push your depth gauge out and your computer will push back in, in its place." I said, "Okay, thanks Eddie" and started carrying everything out to the car. Deb started carrying her dive gear out to the car then we walked back in. We picked out our tanks. I said, "We'll see you later Eddie." Eddie said, "Okay have fun." We carried our tanks to the car then drove to Deb's house. She unloaded her dive gear then I went home and unloaded mine.

Saturday ...

Deb called and said, "We're on our way." I said, "Okay. Is Scott going to stop and let us get something to eat?" Deb said, "Yeah we're hungry."

I started packing my dive gear. They drove up. I loaded all my dive gear into their truck. We were on our way. We stopped and got muffins then drove to Corona Del Mar.

We drove into the parking lot and parked. Scott said, "Deb, look over there" and started pointing at a man and a woman standing next to their car. Deb said, "Oh my gosh." They got out of the truck, started talking to each other then walked over and started talking to them. After a few minutes they walked back to the truck. Deb said, "I can't believe it. That's our neighbors. They just got certified and they're going to do some dives. Can you believe it? We didn't even know they were taking classes." I said, "That's funny."

We ate our muffins then got out and walked over to Ron's truck. Deb said to Ron, "Is there anyway we can go down sooner. When I'm on the surface for very long I get a little seasick." Ron said, "I know I don't like being on the surface for very long either. We should be able to go down sooner. I think it will just be you three today." Deb said, "Thanks Ron. I'm okay after I go down."

Ray and Debbie walked up. Ron said, "What we're going to do on this dive is when I point to you. Hold your alternate air source in your left hand. Then take your regulator out of your mouth with your right hand and blow bubbles the whole time until you put your alternate air source in your mouth and start using it. When I give you the okay signal go ahead and switch back. After everyone does that I want you to pull the top part of your mask away from your face a little bit to let a little bit of water into your mask. Then just blow air out of your nose to drain the water. Then we'll go work on your buoyancy. Go ahead and get your dive gear ready and I'll let everyone know when to put your wetsuit on." We all said okay.

We walked back to the truck and unloaded our dive gear and put it together. A few minutes later Ray walked up and said, "Okay put your wetsuits on and meet on the beach but don't get in until we're all down there.

Deb and I put our wetsuits and dive gear on. We walked to the beach. Ron, Ray and Debbie walked up right after us. Ron said, "Okay air up your BC's. Get with your dive buddy and let's meet at the buoy." Deb and I aired up our BC's, got in the water, put our fins on and started snorkeling out toward the buoy.

We're at the buoy. Ron said to Deb, "Let's check your weight." Deb said, "Okay." She put her regulator in her mouth, grabbed Ron's hand and let the air out of her BC. The water was even with her eyes. She came back up. Ron said, "You're good go ahead and go down." Deb grabbed the buoy anchor line and started down. Ron looked at me and said, "You're next." I put my regulator in my mouth, grabbed Ron's hand and let the air out of my BC. The water level was even with my nose. Ron squeezed my hand. I went back up. Ron said, "You're okay go ahead and go down." I grabbed the buoy anchor line and started going down. I'm slowly going down and equalizing my ears every few feet. The water isn't very clear at all. I looked up. I couldn't see very far. Then I looked down and couldn't see very far. It was an eerie feeling. I kept slowly going down.

I got to the bottom and went over next to Deb and Ray. We could barely see each other and we couldn't see up the anchor line very far at all. We had to stay close to each other to keep from getting separated. Debbie came down, then Ron. Ron came over to me and got in front of me. I thought oh man what am I suppose to do? I had forgotten.

Ron gave me the okay signal. I gave it back. Ron grabbed his alternate air source then took his regulator out of his mouth and pointed to his mouth where he was blowing little bubbles then he put his alternate air source in his mouth. I thought oh yeah this is going to be easy. I took my regulator out of my mouth, blew little bubbles then put my alternate air source in my mouth and started breathing with it. Ron gave me the okay signal. I gave it back. Ron put his regulator back in his mouth. I put mine back in my mouth. Ron went over in front of Deb. We watched Deb while she did it. She didn't have any trouble. Ron went over in front of Debbie. We watched Debbie while she did it. She didn't have any trouble either.

Ron came back in front of me. He pulled the top part of his mask away from his face so a little water could go into his mask. He breathed out of his nose to drain the water then he gave me the okay signal. I gave him the okay signal back and pulled the top of my mask away from my face. I could feel the water running down my face and into my eyes. It wasn't much but it made me a little nervous. I slightly pushed on my mask and blew out of my nose. All the water drained out. Ron went over in front of Deb. We watched Deb while she did it. She didn't have any trouble. Ron went over in front of Debbie. We watched Debbie while she did it. She didn't have any trouble.

Ron pointed with his finger in the direction he wants us to go. Deb got next to Ron on his right side and I got next to Deb. Debbie got on Ron's left side and Ray got next to her. We slowly started going working on our buoyancy. I was getting a little better but not much. I looked over at Ron and could barely see him I couldn't see Ray or Debbie at all.

We kept going along practicing on our buoyancy. Ron started waving at everyone then started pointing at his pressure gauge. He gave each one of us the okay signal. We checked our air and gave him the okay signal back.

We slowly started going again. We kept going looking at the bottom and trying to stay together. Ron waved at us then stopped. We all stopped. Ron pointed at me then pointed for me to go up. I gave him the okay signal and put my power inflator up over my head and started kicking up toward the surface. I'm going up.

I'm on the surface. I aired up my BC. Ray said, "Move over a little so they won't run into you." I said, "Okay" and moved back. Debbie came up and aired up her BC. She moved over close to me. Then Deb and Ron came up.

Ron said, "You're all doing great. Let's get out, change tanks and log our dive." We all said okay and started snorkeling in.

We looked up on the beach. Scott was standing there waiting on us. We could touch now, so we took our fins off and got out. Scott grabbed Deb's fins and mask. He started carrying them. Deb said, "That's so much fun. I can't believe how easy it is to breathe underwater." I said, "I know. It's easy." Scott said, "Did you see any fish?" Deb said, "No you can't see very good. We could barely see each other."

We walked up to the truck and took our dive gear off. We changed tanks, logged our dive and started talking. After awhile we looked over and saw Ray and Debbie at Ron's truck. We walked over to them. Ron said to me, "How did your dive gear work out." I said, "Perfect. I like it." Ron said, "Good I'm sure it'll work out good for you." I said, "Thanks for helping me pick it out."

Ron said, "On our next dive we'll check our air consumption rate. Lee I'll point to my watch and give you five fingers. I want you to time us for five minutes from then. When I give Lee the signal I want everyone to remember their air pressure at that time and also when we stop. Remember both pressures. We'll all have to stay really close together because the visibility is so bad. Go ahead and put your dive gear on and we'll meet on the beach." We all said okay.

We walked back to Scott's truck and put our dive gear on. We saw Ron, Ray and Debbie walking toward the beach so we hurried up and caught up to them. Ray said, "How do you like diving so far?" Deb and I both said we like it. Ray said, "So do I. I go every chance I get. It's okay diving here but it's not the greatest place to do beach dives. The visibility is bad here a lot of the time." I said, "I thought this would be a good place because the tide pools are so good." Ray said, "You would think so."

Ron said, "Okay get your dive buddy and let's meet at the buoy. Don't forget to air up your BC." Deb and I aired up our BC's then walked into the water and put our fins on. We started snorkeling out.

We're at the buoy. Ron said, "Do you guys have the same size tanks?" We all said yes. Ron said, "Good your weight should be okay then." Ron said to me, "Go ahead and go down and stay next to the anchor." I said, "Okay."

I put my regulator in my mouth and reached down and grabbed the buoy anchor line and let the air out of my BC. I was slowly going down and equalizing my ears every few feet.

I'm on the bottom. Ray was already down there. He's looking at me. I went over next to him. Deb came down and got between Ray and I then Debbie came down and got on Ray's other side then Ron came down.

Ron gave everyone the okay signal. We all gave it back. Ron pointed with his finger in the direction he wants us to go. We all got side by side and close together. We're touching shoulders. We started slowly going, working on our buoyancy. Ron pointed at me then pointed at his watch and held five fingers out to me. I gave him the okay signal then checked my dive watch to see what time it is. It's 10:05 and 20 seconds. I checked my air. It was twenty six hundred pounds.

We're staying side by side and close to each other as we were going along the bottom working on our buoyancy. I'm constantly looking at my dive watch. One minute, two minutes, three minutes, four minutes ten seconds, twenty seconds, thirty seconds. Ray went over in front of Ron and started pointing at his dive watch. We all stopped.

Everyone started looking at their pressure gauges. I checked mine. I was down to twenty one hundred pounds. Ron gave everyone the okay signal. We all gave it back. Ron pointed for us to turn around and go back in the direction we came from. We turned around and started back. Ron turned to the right. We turned and stayed next to him. As we were going along it kept getting shallower and shallower. We were at twelve feet. Ron waved at everyone to stop. We all stopped. Ron pointed at me then pointed for me to go up. I gave him the okay signal and started kicking up toward the surface.

I was on the surface next to Ray. I aired up my BC and moved back out of the way. Debbie came up, aired up her BC and moved next to me. Deb and Ron then came up. Ron said, "Don't forget your pressures. Write them down as soon as you get out and also log your dive." We all said okay. Ray and Debbie started snorkeling in. I kicked over to Ron and said, "Hey Ron that wasn't five minutes. It was four minutes and thirty seconds." Ron said, "That's okay. That was close enough." I said, "Okay."

Deb and I started snorkeling in. Scott's standing on the beach waiting on us. We could touch. We took our fins off and got out. Scott grabbed Deb's fins and mask.

We walked up to the truck and took our dive gear off. We wrote down our pressures, logged our dive and then walked over to Ron. Ray and Debbie were talking to Ron. Ron said, "Okay everyone has their start and stop pressures right?" We all said yes. Ron reached in his truck and grabbed a piece of paper and pencil. We told him our pressures. He showed us how to calculate our consumption rate and said, "Go ahead and log your air consumption rate with this dive. That way, later you can check it again and see how much better it's getting. It's usually bad when you're first starting to dive." We all said okay. Ron said, "That will be it for today. Don't forget to get both tanks aired up and clean your dive gear. We'll see you in the morning." We all said okay.

We walked back to Scott's truck and logged our air consumption rate. I said to Scott "Do you feel like taking us to the dive shop to get air." Scott said, "Sure no problem." We took our wetsuits off and loaded our dive gear. We were on our way to the dive shop.

We drove up to the dive shop and carried the tanks in. Eddie was filling tanks. We put ours close to the other ones. Eddie said, "It'll be a little while but I'll get to them." I said, "Okay, thanks Eddie."

We walked up to the front of the dive shop and started looking around. After awhile we walked back to the filling area. Eddie was just getting our tanks full. We loaded the tanks in the truck then Deb and Scott took me home. I unloaded my tanks and dive gear. I said, "You going tomorrow Scott?" Scott said, "Sure. Do you want us to pick you up?" I said, "Sure."

Sunday …

Scott called and said, "We're loaded up. You about ready?" I said, "Yeah, I'm ready." Scott said, "Deb's having a little trouble. She'll tell you about it when we pick you up." I said, "Okay" and thought what in the world kind of trouble could she be having.

They drove up and picked me up. We were on our way to Corona Del Mar. Deb said, "I'm not sure if I'll be able to dive today." I said, "Why not?" Deb said, "It's a monthly curse." I said, "Oh no. Are you going to talk to Ron about it?" Deb said, "Yeah but I would be surprised if he lets me dive." I said, "I will too." We drove through and got breakfast then drove to Corona Del Mar and parked. We looked around the parking lot for Ron. He wasn't there yet.

We ate our breakfast then Ron drove up and parked. We walked over to his truck. Deb said to Ron, "I've got bad news. It's a special time of month for me. Do you think it will be okay for me to dive?" Ron said, "It's your call, but you'll be okay." Deb asked, "Sharks won't get me?" Ron said, "It's very unlikely for a shark to be anywhere near here." Deb said, "Okay I guess I'll go ahead and try it then."

Ray and Debbie walked up. Ron said, "What we'll do on this dive is go down, go along the bottom and work on our buoyancy then we'll imitate doing an emergency ascent at the end of the dive. When the first person gets down to fifteen hundred pounds of air, wave at me then point to your pressure gauge. We'll stop there and do the emergency ascent. The first thing you'll need to do is get on your knees and look at your pressure gauge. I'm going to turn your air off. Watch your pressure go down with every breath you take. When your pressure is low take one last breath until you're out of air. I'm going to open your air back up but don't breathe in. I want you to put your hands on your weight pockets of your BC. That will be how you imitate dumping your weights. Don't dump them just put your hands on them. Also, don't forget I want you to blow bubbles out the whole time. Then I'm going to air up your BC. Go ahead and kick up to the surface but don't forget it's very important to kept blowing bubbles the whole time. Remember no air, blow bubbles, weights. We all said okay. Ron said, "Let's put our dive gear together and we'll suit up soon." We all said okay.

Deb, Scott and I walked back to Scott's truck, unloaded the dive gear and put it together. Ron started waving at us and pointing at his wetsuit while giving us the thumbs up. We gave him the thumbs up back, put our wetsuits on, opened up our air, checked our regulators and put on our dive gear.

We walked over to Ron, Ray and Debbie and walked with them to the beach. Ron said, "Go ahead and air up your BC's and meet at the buoy." We all aired up our BC, got in, put on our fins and mask and started snorkeling toward the buoy.

We were all at the buoy and Ron said, "Does everyone have the same tanks?" We all said yes. Ron said, "Good we won't have to check our weight then." Ron said to Deb, "Go ahead and grab the buoy chain then go down." Deb kicked over to the buoy, put her regulator in her mouth, started letting the air out of her BC and started going down. Ron looked at me and said, "Go ahead Lee." I kicked over to the buoy, put my regulator in my mouth, reached down, grabbed the buoy chain and started letting the air out of my BC. I'm holding the buoy chain and equalizing my ears every few feet down. The visibility is good today. I can see Deb and Ray on the bottom really well. I kept going down.

I'm on the bottom. I went over and got next to Deb. I looked up the chain. Debbie was coming down and Ron was coming down behind her.

They're both on bottom. Ron started pointing. Deb got on Ron's right side and I got next to her. Debbie and Ray got on Ron's left side. We all started going along working on our buoyancy.

Ron started waving at everyone and stopped. He checked everyone's air. Ron started pointing to the left. We turned and started going along the bottom again. Ron started pointing to the left and started turning. We turned with him and kept going. I checked my air. I'm down to fifteen hundred pounds. I started waving at Ron and pointing at my pressure gauge. Ron waved at everyone.

We all stopped and got on our knees. Ron started pointing at my pressure gauge. I looked at it and thought oh yeah, zero air, blow bubbles, weights. I kept looking at my pressure gauge. Ron got next to me. I could feel him shutting my air valve. I started getting nervous. I kept watching my air pressure go down with every breath I took. Okay this is my last breath I'm breathing in. The air stopped, my pressure gauge is on zero. I started blowing little bubbles out of my mouth and put my hands on my weight pockets. I can feel Ron opening my air valve. He started airing up my BC. I started going up. I started kicking up toward the surface. I kept blowing out bubbles.

I'm on the surface. Ray grabbed me. I can feel him turning my air valve. Ray said, "Go ahead and air up your BC all the way. Ron just cracked your air valve open in case you needed to breathe but I just opened it all the way." I shook my head yes, aired up my BC and moved back out of the way. I took my regulator out of my mouth.

Ray started looking down at the bottom then started moving around. Deb came up next to him. Ray grabbed her and opened her air valve. Deb moved back next to me and took her regulator out of her mouth. Debbie came up then Ron right after her. Ron took his regulator out of his mouth and said, "Okay lets get out, change tanks and log our dive then meet at my truck in a little while." We all said okay and started kicking in.

We can see Scott on the beach. We started waving at him. He waved back and started walking toward us. We can touch bottom. We took our fins off and got out. Scott grabbed Deb's fins and mask. We walked to Scott's truck. We changed tanks, logged our dive and then sat on the tailgate of the truck.

We sat around talking for awhile then we walked over to Ron's truck. Ray and Debbie were talking to Ron. Ron looked at Deb and I and said, "Are we having fun yet?" We answered yes. Ron said, "Good, on your next dive you and your dive buddy need to decide on a dive plan. Then go and do it. You're on your own. When you come back, I want you to come over and talk to me. Everyone should come back with at least five hundred pounds of air." Deb said, "Can we just go out a little way then go down or do we have to go down at the buoy?" Ron said, "However you and your dive buddy want to do it. It's your dive. Have fun and be careful. I'll see you when you get back." Deb said, "Oh good this is going to be fun." I said, "Yeah it is."

Deb, Scott and I started walking back to Scott's truck. Deb looked over at me and said, "Let's just go out a little way then go down." I said, "Okay lets go down then go toward the tidepools." Deb said, "Okay."

We walked up to the truck and went over to our dive gear. We opened up our air and checked our regulators. Deb asked if I was about ready to put my dive gear on. I said I was ready. We put on our dive gear then I walked around Deb looking at her dive gear. I told her that her dive gear looked good. Deb walked around me looking at my dive gear and said, "Yours does too." Deb said, "I'm ready if you are." I said, "I'm ready but I'm a little nervous." Deb said, "Me too."

We started walking toward the beach. Scott's carrying Deb's mask and fins for her. We were getting close to the water. I said, "We need to air up our BC's." We both aired them up. Scott handed Deb her mask and fins. We walked into the water, put our fins on and started kicking out. Deb said, "We're just going to go out some, go down and then go that way." She was pointing down the beach toward the tidepools. I said, "Yeah, we need to set our compass heading in that direction." We both started setting our compasses. Deb said, "When are we going to turn around and come back?" I said, "We've got three thousand pounds of air so why don't we turn around at two thousand pounds. Then if we have a lot of air when we get back here we can look around." Deb said, "Okay." I asked if she was ready to go down. Deb said, "Yeah I'm ready."

We put our masks on and put our regulators in our mouths. We looked at each other and shook our heads yes. We slowly started letting the air out of our BC's. We were already on the bottom. We got on our knees and faced each other. We were only nine feet deep. We checked our air and gave each other the okay signal.

I looked at my compass and pointed in the direction of the tidepools. Deb gave me the okay signal. We slowly started going. We were close to the bottom working on our buoyancy. We were going along almost constantly looking at our compasses and pressure gauges and only taking a quick look at each other and around. We were going along nice and slow.

There's a rock in front of us about the size of a coffee table. We went up to it, stopped and started looking at it. We went all the way around it, looking at it. It has algae like stuff growing on it and a little fish swimming next to it. We checked our compasses and started going again. We're not seeing much, just a sandy bottom and that one rock. I checked my air. I'm down to two thousand pounds. I looked at Deb and pointed to my pressure gauge. I pointed for us to turn around and start back. Deb gave me the okay signal.

We turned around and started going back. We kept watching our compasses and air pressure. We kept going along real slow. Deb started waving at me and pointing in front of us. It was a flounder about ten inches long swimming along the sandy bottom. We watched it swim away.

I checked my air. I'm down to a thousand pounds. We were fifteen feet deep. I waved at Deb and pointed at my pressure gauge then pointed up to the surface. Deb gave me the okay signal. We got close together and started going up.

We were on the surface. We aired up our BC's and took our regulators out of our mouths. I said, "I wasn't sure how far we came back so I thought we should go up and look around." Deb said, "I was wondering the same thing." I said, "I still have nine hundred pounds of air. How much do you have?" Deb said, "Sixteen hundred pounds." I said, "Man you have a lot of air." Deb asked, "Why did you use yours so fast?" I said, "I don't know. Why don't we set our compasses, go toward the beach where we came in at and when I have seven hundred pounds of air, go up." Deb said, "Okay but don't go under five hundred pounds or we'll get in trouble." I said, "Okay."

We set our compasses, put our regulators back in our mouths and let the air out of our BC's. We're on the bottom. We looked at our compasses and started in. We were going along real slow. I was at seven hundred pounds. We were ten feet deep. I looked at Deb and pointed up. Deb gave me the okay signal.

We went up, aired up our BC's and took our regulators out of our mouths. Deb said, "Man that's fun." I said, "It sure is." Deb started looking around and said, "There's Scott." He's down the beach a little way looking in the wet sand for shells. Deb hollered out really loud, "Hi hon. There's my honey." Scott started waving and walking toward us. We kicked in to where we could touch, took our fins off and got out.

Deb started walking toward Scott. I started walking toward the truck. I walked up to the truck and started taking my dive gear off. I can hear Deb and Scott talking to Ray and Debbie. I looked up at them. Scott's wearing Deb's dive gear and carrying her mask and fins. Debbie and Ray walked over to Ray's truck.

Deb and Scott walked up. Scott started taking Deb's dive gear off. Deb and I took our wetsuits off. We packed everything in the truck then started walking toward Ron. Ron was talking to Debbie and looked at us and yelled, "Bring your dive logs." We gave him the okay signal, turned around and went back to get them. We handed Ron our dive logs. Ron said, "How was it?" Deb and I both said, "It was a lot of fun." Deb said, "We saw a rock, a little fish and a flounder." Ron said, "Good. I'm glad you saw something." Ron started looking through our dive logs and started signing them. He said, "Okay that's it. You guys are certified. Be careful out there." Deb said, "We're certified divers?" Ron said, "Yes you are. I'm happy to say you are now certified divers." Deb said, "That wasn't very hard at all." I said, "No it wasn't but I sure am hungry now." Ron said, "There's some fast food places next to the freeway you'll see them right before you get on it." I said, "Let's go eat Ron, I'll buy you lunch." Deb said, "We'll pitch in too." Debbie said, "I will too." Ron said, "Okay, lets go have lunch but it'll be my treat. You guys have been a great class. Do you guys like Mexican food?" We all said yes. I looked at Ron and said, "We'll buy you lunch Ron you've been a great instructor." Ron started laughing and said, "Follow me."

We all got in our cars and followed Ron. We drove up to the Mexican food restaurant, parked and walked in. We all ordered. We all tried to pay but Ron wouldn't let us and paid for everything. We all sat down and ate.

We walked out to the parking lot and said bye. Deb, Scott and I got in Scott's truck and started home. Deb said, "When are we going diving?" I said, "My day off is Friday. I've got to work graveyards until then." Deb said, "Friday's fine. I talked to Ray. He told me we should try diving at a place called Shaw's Cove. He said it's better than Corona Del Mar and it's just a few miles further down the coast. All we have to do is go to Laguna Beach to Beverly Street. He said there's a dive shop where you turn. You turn right and run right into it" I said, "Okay that sounds good to me." Deb said, "David told me I can use his dive gear anytime I want as long as he's not using it but he wants to use it first to check it out." I said, "Good, I think it's been a while since he went diving so that's probably a good idea."

We drove up to my house. I unloaded my dive gear. Deb and Scott went home. I cleaned my dive gear and put it up.

I called David and said, "Deb and I are certified divers." David said, "Good. When are we going diving?" I said, "That's funny Deb just asked me the same thing. We're planning on going Friday. Do you want to go?" David said, "No, I'm going dancing Friday and Saturday but how about Sunday?" I said, "Okay." David said, "Lets just do one dive and see how it goes." I said, "Okay. What are you guys doing?" David said, "We just finished eating and now I think I'll get my dive gear out and check it. Come over and take a look at it." I said, "Okay I'll be right over."

I drove to David and mom's and walked in. David has his dive gear spread out on the living room floor. He's looking at everything and checking it out. I picked up his BC and started looking at it. It doesn't have an alternate air source. I said, "The dive shop will frown on you if you dive without a alternate air source." David said, "If I have any trouble I'll just go up. They made us go up from a hundred feet without air to get certified." I said, "You're kidding. I'm glad they didn't make us do that. I don't think I would have made it." I looked at his pressure gauge and said, "I bought a computer and they threw in a console with a compass and a pressure gauge." David said, "I'm going to get a compass one of these days." We both checked out his dive gear. Everything looked good and worked fine. I went back home.

Monday …

Deb called and said, "You ready to take your tanks back?" I said, "Yeah." Deb said, "I'm going to go buy that wetsuit I was looking at." I said, "Okay, I'll be over in a little bit." I loaded my tanks, drove over, picked Deb and her dive gear up. We were on our way to the dive shop.

Deb said, "You know what? I'll have everything but a BC, tank and regulators. If I rent them from the dive shop it will be easy for all three of us to go diving." I said, "That's a good idea. Surely it won't cost much to rent a BC, tank and regulators."

We drove up and parked in the back. I carried my tanks to the filling area. Deb started putting her dive gear up. I walked back to the car and carried Deb's tanks to the filling area. We walked up to the front. Eddie was busy. I said to Eddie, "We're just going to look around." Eddie said, "Okay, let me know if you have any questions."

Deb found the wetsuit she liked and put it on the counter and said, "I went over and looked at David's dive gear last night. He doesn't have an integrated BC and I didn't like his weight belt. It's hard to take the weights on and off so I'm going to look at the weight belts too." I said, "I went over there too." Deb said, "They said you just left when we got there." Deb started looking at the weight belts and said, "I like this one" then she picked up the weights to go with it.

Deb tried on some gloves and said, "I like these" then walked over and looked at the hoods. I said, "I got this hooded vest." Deb said, "I'm just going to get this hood so I don't go over my budget." Deb put all her stuff on the counter. Eddie walked up and said, "Sorry I've been a little busy but I'm caught up now. Anything I can help you with?" Deb said, "I would like to buy this stuff." I said, "I would like to order another power inflator with a back up regulator built into it like the one I have." Eddie said, "Okay, It'll take a couple of days to get it. We'll call you when it comes in." I said, "Okay."

Deb paid for all of her stuff and then I paid for mine. Deb said to Eddie, "Would it cost much to rent a BC, tank and regulators?" Eddie said, "It cost the same amount to rent one thing or the entire dive gear. But since you guys took the dive classes, you can borrow the dive gear for a few dives, no charge. They actually would rather that you don't rent the equipment because they want it for the students." Deb said, "Okay I'll just need to borrow a BC, tank and regulators a few times." Eddie said, "That won't be any problem." Deb said, "Thanks, Eddie."

We loaded everything in the car then drove to Deb's house. She unloaded all her dive gear then I drove home.

Wednesday ...

Eddie called and left me a message, "Hey Lee, your power inflator with the backup regulator just came in. You can pick it up anytime you would like." I woke up and checked my messages then drove to the dive shop and walked in. Eddie said, "You must have gotten my message" and handed me a box. I said, "I did" and opened up the box and said, "That's it. Thanks Eddie." I drove back home.

I called David and said, "Are you going to be home for awhile." David said, "Yeah, come on over." I said, "Okay. I'll be right there." I drove to David's and walked in. I said, "I bought you something" and handed him the power inflator with the backup regulator. David said, "You shouldn't have bought me that." I said, "I didn't. I bought it for me. If I run out of air, I'll use it. Not really if I run out of air, you'll need it. I won't do like the dive shop taught us to go up to your buddy and give the out of air signal. Then wait on them to change regulators. I'm just going to take your regulator then you'll know I'm out of air when your regulator is in my mouth." I started laughing and said, "Yeah, that's my signal. You'll know I'm out of air when you don't have a regulator in your mouth." David started smiling and probably thought I was joking.

David said, "How do I put it on?" I said, "I don't know but I think you just put it on with two wire ties. That's how they put mine on." David went and got two wire ties from his room and strapped the power inflator to his low-pressure hose on his BC. David hooked up his high-pressure hose to it from his first stage regulator then breathed in and out through the regulator part. Then he aired up his BC and let the air out and said, "Seems to be working okay." I said, "Good." We sat around talking for awhile then I went home.

Chapter 2

Diving on our own

Thursday ...

I called Deb and asked, "You ready to go get your dive gear?" Deb said, "Yeah pick me up." I said, "Okay. I'm on my way." I drove to Deb's house and picked her up then we drove to the dive shop. We walked in and walked up to the front. Eddie was behind the counter. Deb asked, "Can I borrow a BC, regulators and two tanks?" Eddie said, "Sure." I said, "I too, would like to borrow two tanks." Eddie said, "Sure, we should get your tanks in pretty soon." Eddie walked over and got Deb's dive gear. Deb and I grabbed four tanks. Deb and I said thanks to Eddie and loaded everything in the car. I took Deb home. She unloaded her dive gear. I went home and unloaded my tanks.

Friday ...

I called Deb and said, "Let's go." Deb said, "Okay, pick me up." I loaded my dive gear in the car and drove to Deb's house. She loaded her dive gear. We were on our way to Shaw's Cove. I said, "We're on our own." Deb said, "I know. I can't believe it." I started thinking we're certified but it sure doesn't seem like we know what we're doing very well.

We started getting close. Deb said, "There's the dive shop" and started pointing in front of us. I drove up to it and made a right turn. We drove to the end of the small street. Deb said, "There it is" and started pointing at some steps. We parked and walked over to the steps. It was a small area with steps going down to the beach. Deb said, "Let's go take a look." I said, "Okay." We walked down to the beach and looked around. It's a nice little beach with a reef on both sides and small waves breaking on the shore. Deb said, "This looks like a nice place." I said, "It does." Deb said, "Let's go." We walked back up to the car.

We unloaded all of our dive gear onto the street behind the car and started putting it all together. Every now and then we would see some divers coming out from the small area that comes from the beach. Almost all of them looked really tired.

We had our dive gear together. We opened up our air and started breathing through our regulators checking them out. Everything worked fine. Deb started discussing our dive plan. She asked me what I thought about going out, looking at the reef and then start back in when our pressure was down to fifteen hundred pounds. I said, "Okay, that sounds good to me."

Deb asked if I was ready to start putting on my wetsuit. I told her that I was ready. We both had our bathing suits on under our clothes. That made it easy, so then all we had to do is take off our clothes and put on our wetsuits. We barely got our wetsuits on and we were already starting to get hot.

We helped each other put our dive gear on. Then we checked each other's dive gear just like they taught us. Deb said, "Let's go I'm hot." I said, "Me too. Let's go!"

We walked over to the steps then down to the beach. We started getting close to the water. I said, "Don't forget to air up your BC." I aired mine up then Deb did the same. We got into the water and put on our fins. We kicked out a little way. Deb asked, "Do you want to go down now?" I responded, "Yeah let's go down then toward the reef." I looked at the reef and set the heading marker on my compass to point toward the reef. The reef was only a little bit away from us.

We both put on our mask and put our regulators in our mouths then started to let the air out of our BC's. We were staying really close to each other. We were slowly going down, popping our ears on the way. When we got down to the sandy bottom, we got on our knees. We were ten feet deep.

We were looking around. The visibility was good. We could see a lot farther than we had ever seen before, twenty feet at least. We gave each other the okay hand signal. I looked at my compass and pointed in the direction of the reef. We started kicking in that direction. We were kicking along the sandy bottom, staying a foot or two from it. We were going slow, working on our buoyancy and kept giving each other the okay hand signal. We saw a couple of little flounder type fish that were only about ten inches long. We were pointing at everything we could see.

I looked up ahead of us and could see something black and square. I poked Deb in her side with my finger and pointed at it. We started toward it. It was a big boom-box radio sitting on the bottom. It was in pretty good shape for being on the ocean floor! It looked like it had only been down there a couple of days. We started toward the reef again, slowly proceeding while looking around.

We saw something small moving over the sand about five feet from our left so we stopped and started watching it. It was a small creature. It kept going and went right in front of us! It was walking on top of the sand just a couple of feet in front of us. We pointed at it while it was moving past us. It looked like a mouse without a tail. We watched it for awhile and then started going toward the reef again.

After a few more minutes, I was thinking we should have been at the reef by now. I looked at Deb and pointed at my eyes then pointed up, meaning that I'd like for us to go up and look around. She gave me the okay hand signal. We slowly started up. We got to the surface, aired up our BC's and took our regulators out of our mouths. We were a long way away from the reef now. I must have been looking at the wrong heading marker on the compass. I told Deb, "I can't believe it! I had us going in the wrong direction." Deb said, "I can't believe it either." I said, "I thought we should have been there already. I'll try to do it right this time. Are you ready to go the right way?" Deb said, "Yeah, let's go." I double-checked the compass and said, "Okay."

I looked at the reef, then at my compass. We put our regulators back in our mouths, started letting the air out of our BC's and started back down. I kept looking at the compass this time. When we got to the bottom I pointed toward the reef. We started toward it but this time we were going faster. We were kicking along, staying a foot or two off the bottom while working on our buoyancy.

After a few minutes, we could see something big and dark ahead of us. We started slowing down. I was getting nervous. Then I realized that it was the reef. We were fifteen feet deep. The reef is a big huge rock from the bottom to the surface with plants and all kinds of stuff growing on it. There were several fish around it, including these big orange fish that were about eight inches long.

We started going out next to the reef. We were trying to look at everything on it! It was like the whole thing was alive when we looked closely at it. You could see that everything was some kind of plant or tiny animal. We kept on all the while going deeper and deeper, still looking at it.

We were at forty-nine feet. I checked my air. I was down to fifteen hundred pounds. Deb checked hers. She still had twenty one hundred pounds! I pointed back toward shore. Deb gave me the okay sign. We turned around and started in, looking at the reef as we were going.

We were at ten feet when I started having trouble staying on the bottom. I was floating up. I let out all of the air in my BC and still couldn't stay down. I was floating up to the surface.

I was on the surface so I aired up my BC. Deb came up right after me. We took our regulators out of our mouths and our masks off. I said, "I couldn't stay down for some reason." Deb said, "I was wondering what you were doing. That mouse thing looked so cute! It looked just like a mouse." I said, "It did. I wonder what it was? That radio looked weird too and so did those big orange fish. What do you think they are?" Deb said, "Those are garibaldi. Aren't they neat?" I said, "Yeah, they are like giant goldfish."

We were out in the water floating around while resting for a bit. Then I asked Deb if she was ready to get out. Deb said that she was so we kicked in toward the area where the small waves were breaking and took off our fins. We then got out of the water. We walked across the beach and started up the steps.

Deb stopped and hunched over facing forward. She said, "I can't make it. I'm too tired!" I said, "You'll make it. It's not too much further now." Then all of a sudden she took off really fast. She walked up a few more steps then once again stopped and hunched over forward while saying, "I can't make it. I'm really too tired." I said, "Yes you will. We're really getting close now." We kept doing the same thing over and over until finally we managed to make it to the top of the steps. Deb looked at the car and sighed, "Oh no! Look how far it is!"

We made our way over to the car. Deb exclaimed, "Man! I'm really tired now! That was a long way back." I said, "I'm tired too. At least it was downhill going which made it easier." We took off our dive gear and wetsuits then dried off. We rested for awhile then got out our dive logs and logged our dive.

We changed our tanks. I asked Deb if she was ready to do our next dive. Deb replied that she was. We started putting our wetsuits back on. They were wet, cold and sandy. We managed to get them on, in spite of all that. We were getting hot really fast. We opened up our air and checked our regulators. I put my dive gear on then helped Deb put hers on.

We walked to the steps and started down them. I said, "Boy it's a lot easier to walk down the steps rather than up them!" Deb responded sarcastically, "Yeah. I can't wait to come back!" We walked down the steps and started walking across the beach. Deb said, "Man, am I hot." I replied that I was too.

We were getting close to the water. Deb said, "Let's get in. It's cooler in the water." I said, "Okay, air up your BC." We aired up our BC's and hurried up, got in and kicked out a little way. Deb said, "Oh, this is nice. Let's rest a little. I never thought I would be glad to get into cold water!" I replied, "I know what you mean! This feels good."

We floated around awhile then kicked out to where we went down on the first dive, before I had us go the wrong way. Deb said, "Don't get us lost." I said, "Okay but if we don't get there soon we're probably going the wrong way again. It's not that far." Deb asked, "You ready?" I said, "Yeah, let me set my good old dependable compass." I set it then said, "Let's go."

We put our mask on, our regulators in our mouths and started letting the air out of our BC's. We were both slowly going down while popping our ears along the way. We made it to the sandy bottom and got on our knees. We gave each other the okay signal.

I carefully checked my compass. I'm sure it's the right direction this time. I pointed in the direction toward the reef. Deb gave me the okay signal.

We were slowly going along about a foot or two off the bottom. Then Deb quickly veered to the right like she was going to look at something. I started following her. She stopped and started looking down at the sand. I went over, next to her.

It's a hole in the sand breathing. I'm thinking oh my gosh what is this thing? It's a hole about the size of a fifty cent piece, breathing. We could tell it was breathing by the way the water was moving the sand on the edges of the hole. I'm thinking it must be some kind of fish buried under the sand but how? All the sand around it was smooth and flat like it hasn't been disturbed for a long time.

Deb pointed at me with her finger like she was going to poke it. I quickly shook my head no and extended my arms and hands out showing her that it could be five or six feet long. Deb looked disappointed. We watched it some more then left it alone and started going toward the reef. After we had been going along for a little while, I started thinking it must have been a flounder and that would have been okay to poke. I started waving at Deb. We both stopped. I drew two lines that bowed out and touched on the ends to look like what I thought a flounder would look like. Deb looked at me and gave me a strange look. She didn't know what I was drawing. I tried to fix it up a little better. She still gave me that strange look. I gave up and started pointing for us to keep going. We started going.

We could see the dark outline from the reef coming up. We got to the reef and started going along it looking all over it again. We kept going out. We were at sixty feet. My air was down to fifteen hundred pounds so I signaled to Deb. We turned around and started back in. We kept looking at the reef on the way back.

We were at ten feet and I couldn't stay down again. I was floating up. I signaled to Deb to go up. She gave me the okay signal. We went up. We got on the surface, aired up our BC's, took our regulators out of our mouths and our mask off.

Deb said, "What was that you drew in the sand?" I said, "A flounder." Deb said, "Oh my gosh two lines is a flounder? I can't believe that was a flounder." She started laughing then said, "Do you think that breathing hole was a flounder? It sure was weird?" I said, "I was thinking it probably was but I wasn't sure. It was weird. I wonder how big it was?" Deb said, "I don't know but it was pretty big." I said, "I can't believe you were going to poke it!" Deb said, "I wanted to see it."

We kept floating around, resting and I said, "You ready to get out?" Deb said, "Not really but I guess if we have to." We kicked in close, took our fins off and got out. Deb said, "I'll never make it." I said, "Give me your weights and I'll carry them." Deb said, "Oh good." We walked across the beach and started up the steps. Deb did the same thing, hunching over and resting, then taking off, over and over all the way up the steps. We finally made it back to the car. Deb said, "Oh, I'm tired." I said, "Me too. I'm hot and tired." We took off our dive gear and wetsuits then loaded everything in the car.

We were on our way to Deb's house. Deb said, "When are we going diving next?" I said, "I'm going with David on Sunday. So pick a day." Deb said, "How about the following Saturday? I said, "Sounds good to me but I work days so it will have to be after I get off work." Deb said, "Okay, I don't want to get up early anyway." We drove up to Deb's house. She unloaded her dive gear. I drove home, unloaded mine, cleaned it and put it up.

Saturday …

I called David and asked, "We're still going tomorrow, right?" David said, "Yeah but I've got to air up my tank." I said, "I've got to take my loaner tanks back. I'll take yours and get it aired up if you want me too." David said, "Okay and just keep it until tomorrow." I said, "Okay. I'll be over in a little bit."

I called Deb and said, "Are you ready to take your dive gear back?" Deb said, "Yeah." I said, "I'm going to pick up David's tank then I'll be over." I loaded my tanks in the car then went and picked up David's. I drove to Deb's. I picked her and her dive gear up.

We drove to the dive shop. I started carrying the tanks in and setting them down at the filling area. Deb put her dive gear up. Eddie was working on some dive gear. I said, "Is there any way that I can get this tank filled? It's my brother's. Also, can I borrow a full tank?" Eddie said, "Sure no problem" and walked over and started filling David's tank along with one I brought in. Eddie said, "Just so you know, the tank fills are free until you get your tanks. Then you'll have to start paying for them to be filled." I said, "That's no problem. Did I see that it costs about three or four dollars to fill them?" Eddie said, "Yes, for one fill. But if you buy a dive card, it's ten fills for ten dollars." I said, "You're kidding! That's only a dollar a fill! That's not bad at all." Eddie had the tanks full. I said, "Thanks Eddie."

Deb and I carried the tanks to the car and loaded them. I drove Deb home then I went home and unloaded the tanks.

Sunday ...

I called David and asked, "You ready to go diving?" David said, "Yeah. I'll be right over." I asked him if he wanted to go to Shaw's Cove. David said, "Okay." I asked, "Do you want me to drive?" David said, "I can drive. I've got my dive gear already packed in the truck." I said, "Okay, I'll be ready when you get here." I packed up all my dive gear along with the two tanks and put everything on the front porch. David drove up. We loaded my dive gear and the tanks in his truck. We were on our way to Shaw's Cove.

We drove up to Shaw's Cove and started looking for a parking spot. It was crowded. Divers were all around walking back and forth across the street, to and from the steps, and putting on their dive gear behind their cars. We couldn't find a parking spot. David said, "Is there any where else where we can go in at?" I said, "There must be." David said, "Lets drive around and see."

We drove down the little street a few blocks, found a parking spot then got out and started looking down toward the ocean. David started pointing and said, "That looks like a trail. Look there's even divers over there." I responded, "Yeah! This looks like a good place." David said, "Let's try it."

We unloaded all of our dive gear and put it behind the truck. We started putting it all together. David said, "I hope I don't have any trouble with my dive gear. It's been a while since I've used it." I said, "It will probably be okay." We opened up our air and checked our regulators. Everything seemed okay.

I said, "We're supposed to have a dive plan. I'll just follow you. With Deb we turned around and started back in when either one of us got down to fifteen hundred pounds." David said, "That sounds good to me." I said, "Let me know when you're ready to put your wetsuit on because you get really hot after you put it on." David said, "I'm ready if you are."

We started putting on our wetsuits. David said, "Oh man! My hood is tight and I can't get it tucked in the back. Can you tuck it in for me?" I said, "Sure" and tucked it in. David said, "You're right. I'm really hot. Let's hurry up." I said, "Okay."

We put our dive gear on then walked over to the start of the trail. It was a steep dirt trail that winded down to a little beach area. I said, "Man, you better not slip." David said, "Yeah, really!" We slowly started walking down it.

We finally made it to the bottom then started walking toward the water. I asked, "Are you ready to get in?" David said, "Yeah, I'm hot! Air up your BC and let's get in." We both aired up our BC's, got into the water, put our fins on and kicked out a little way. David asked, "You ready to go down?" I said, "Yeah. I'm ready."

We put our masks on and our regulators in our mouths. We started letting the air out of our BC's. We were going down slow staying next to each other. We got on the sandy bottom and were on our knees. We gave each other the okay signal.

David started going along about a foot or two off the bottom. I stayed right behind him. There were big rocks around, just like at Shaw's Cove, but there wasn't as much marine life on them for some reason. We kept going out deeper, looking around but not seeing much.

We were at fifty-five feet. I had fifteen hundred pounds of air. I grabbed David's fin. He turned around and looked at me. I pointed at my pressure gauge then pointed in. David gave me the okay signal, turned around and started in.

I kept following him. We were at twenty feet. I still had eight hundred pounds of air. I signaled David with eight fingers while pointing at my pressure gauge to show him how much air I still had. He gave me the okay signal.

We went over and started looking at these two big rocks that are close together, with a big crack between them. I looked into the crack. There's an old car tire sitting in it. I was surprised. It was so clean everywhere then there's this old tire.

I was starting to have trouble staying down, close to the bottom. I checked my air. I'm down to five hundred pounds. I signaled to David for us to start going up. He gave me the okay signal. We started going up.

When we got to the surface, we aired up our BC's, took our regulators out of our mouths and took off our masks. David said, "That was fun but we sure didn't see much." I said, "I know. Shaw's Cove is a lot better." David said, "I didn't have any trouble with my dive gear. It seems to be okay."

We floated around for awhile then David asked, "You ready to get out?" I said, "Yeah. I'm ready." We kicked in to where we could touch and took our fins off. Then we got out of the water. We started walking up the trail. I said, "I hope we don't slip now since our booties are wet." David said, "Me too." We walked up the trail and over to the truck. We took off our dive gear and wetsuits. We loaded everything in the truck.

We were on our way home. I asked, "When are we going diving next?" David said, "I can't go until Saturday." I said, "Deb and I planned on going Saturday. Let's all three go." David said, "Okay." I said, "I work days so it will have to be after I get home from work. Do you want to do two dives." David said, "Yeah, that sounds good to me."

We drove up to my house. I unloaded my dive gear and said, "Do you want me to fill your tank?" David said, "Sure. Just let me know what I owe you." I said, "Since we have tanks ordered they fill them for free. After that, we can buy dive cards for ten dollars and get ten fills." David said, "That's a good deal. That's the cheapest I've ever heard of." I said, "I know. It's cheap." David went home.

I cleaned my dive gear and put it up. I walked into the house and called Deb. I told her that David was going with us on Saturday. Deb responded that it would be fun.

Monday …

I loaded the tanks in the car and drove to the dive shop. I carried the tanks in and put them at the filling area next to two blue tanks and a white tank. I walked up to the front. Ron was behind the counter. Ron looked over at me and said, "Hey, your tanks just came in a few minutes ago. I was about to call you." I said, "I saw some in the back. Is that them?" Ron said, "Yes. They're full. I just finished filling them." I said, "Good, thanks." Ron said, "I just checked on your computer too. It should be here today or tomorrow." I said, "Sounds good." Ron said, "There's still room on the Catalina trip next Monday. We're going to do a deep dive. Do you want to go?" We both looked up at the dry erase board on the wall. There are three openings left. Ron said, "There's three left and it usually fills up." I said, "That is my day off. Yeah, I'll go." Ron said, "On the first dive we'll be doing a deep dive to a hundred feet. We'll certify you as a deep diver on it." I said, "That sounds like fun." Ron said, "It is. It's a lot of fun diving at Catalina. They're nothing like the beach dives we do over here. Wait until you see the visibility." I said, "I can't wait." Ron said, "We always have a good time at Catalina." I said, "I'll ask Deb and David if they want to go."

Ron and I walked back to the filling area. Ron aired up David's tank. I thanked Ron and loaded all four tanks in the car then headed home.

I unloaded my two tanks. I went inside and called Deb and asked her if she wanted to go on the Catalina dive trip Monday with the dive shop. Deb said, "I would like to but I have to work." I said, "Okay."

I called David and asked him if he was going to be home for awhile. I told him that I had something for him. David said that he was going to be there all day. So, I drove to David's and carried in his tanks. I said, "The tanks just came in." David said, "Good." I said, "I'm going with the dive shop to Catalina on Monday. Do you want to go?" David said, "I'd like to but I better not." I said, "Sounds like it's going to be fun." David said, "Maybe next time." We talked awhile then I went home.

Tuesday …

Ron called and said, "Your computer is in." I said, "Good. I'll be right there." I went and grabbed my depth gauge and regulators. I drove to the dive shop and walked up to the front. Ron was behind the counter. I put my depth gauge and regulators on the counter and asked, "Can you help me put it in?" Ron said, "Sure, it's easy. I'll show you." He twisted the rubber console and pulled out the depth gauge then he pushed the computer into the console and said, "That's all there is to it." I said, "That looked easy. Thanks Ron." I went home and put my regulators and computer with my dive gear.

Friday …

Deb called and left me a message saying that she had her dive gear. She said that Scott had helped her pick it up.

Saturday …

David called and asked, "Are you about ready?" I said, "Yeah. Do you want me to drive?" David said, "That is what I was thinking. If I drive we'll all be crowded. It will probably be better if we go in your car." I said, "That is what I was thinking. I'll be over in a little bit."

I called Deb and asked her if she was ready. Deb stated that she was and asked me to come and pick her up. I told her that I was going to get David, and then I'd be over. I loaded my dive gear, went to pick up David and his dive gear, and then went to pick up Deb along with her dive gear.

We were on our way to Shaw's Cove. I said, "How about this for our dive plan … we go out the reef and start back in when anyone gets down to fifteen hundred pounds." Deb and David both said, "Sounds good to me." I said, "David since you know more about diving why don't you lead with Deb following you and I'll follow Deb." Deb and David said okay.

We started getting close. Deb said, "I thought I saw a wave. I hope the surf isn't big." I said, "Me too." We drove to Shaw's Cove and found a parking spot. It wasn't very crowded and there was a lot of parking spaces.

We got out of the car and could hear the waves crashing. Deb said, "Eeek! The waves sound big!" I said, "Let's go look at them." We walked down the steps to where we could see the waves. They're big, but they didn't look too big. I said, "All we have to do is hurry up and get past the break and we'll be okay." Deb said, "Yeah I hope so."

We walked back to the car, unloaded our dive gear and started putting it together. We opened up our air and checked our regulators. Deb said, "Let's all put our wetsuits on at the same time to keep from getting too hot." I said, "Okay." David said, "I'm ready when you guys are." I said, "Let's put them on." David said, "Can you help me with my hood?" I said, "Sure" and went over and tucked it in for him then put my dive gear on.

We were all ready. Deb said, "Let's go." We walked over to the steps then down to the beach. We were a little way from the water and David said, "Be sure you air up your BC's." We all aired them up. I said, "We need to time the waves. Usually there are two or three big ones then a few smaller ones. We need to go right after the big ones." We started watching the waves. David said, "Lee tell us when." I said, "Okay I'll let you know." A big wave came in then another one. The next ones looked small. I said, "Now."

We all hurried up, got in the water, put our fins on and started kicking out. I could see a big wave not too far out. I told Deb, "Hurry, hurry, hurry." We were all hurrying. I reached over, grabbed Deb's air valve on her tank and started pulling her out. We made it out just past where the waves were breaking.

We slowed down and kicked out a little further then Deb said, "I'm ready to go down." David and I said we were ready too. We all got close to each other and put our masks on and our regulators in our mouth. We started letting the air out of our BC's and started going down, popping our ears along the way. When we got to the sandy bottom, we all got on our knees and gave each other the okay signal. We were sixteen feet deep.

We were really close to the reef. David started first, then Deb, and finally me. The visibility wasn't very good. It was only about ten feet, if that much, and there was a little bit of surging pulling us out a little, then pushing us back in. We were going along, following each other. We started looking in the cracks on the reef, and all over it, looking at the fish and plants.

We came up to an opening where we could go in two different directions. David went straight ahead. Deb turned and went to the right. I stopped. David kept going gradually fading out of sight. Deb kept going gradually fading out of sight. I stayed still and waited hoping they would turn around and come back.

After a couple of minutes David came back. I pointed in the direction that Deb went then started going in that direction. David was following me. We found Deb. She was looking at an animal in a crack in the reef. David and I started looking around too.

I checked my air. I'm down to fifteen hundred pounds. I signaled to David and Deb for us to start back in. They gave me the okay signal. I started going. I was in front then Deb. David was last. We were looking at the reef on our way in. We were still surging back and forth a little. The shallower we got, the worse the surge was getting. I pointed up. Deb and David gave me the okay signal.

We went up. When we were on the surface we aired up our BC's, took our regulators out of our mouths and took our masks off. I asked Deb, "What happened? You didn't follow David. You went into that opening." Deb said, "I thought I saw some fish in there and wanted to take a look at them." I said, "I thought we were going to get separated."

We started looking at the waves. I said, "We need to time them again and when we start in, we need to hurry." We started watching the waves. A big one went past us, then another one. I said, "Now." We all started kicking in fast. Some smaller waves were breaking and pushing us in. We could touch. We took our fins off and got out of the water.

I told Deb to give me her weights and I would carry them for her. She took them off and handed them to me. We walked to the steps and started up them. I was following Deb and David was behind me. Deb stopped and rested, then took off every few steps just like before. We finally made it up the steps and to the car. We took off our dive gear and wetsuits. We dried off. We changed tanks and logged our dives. We sat around talking and resting.

After awhile David said, "I'm ready when you guys are." Deb and I said that we were ready. David said, "This time how about Deb lead, then Lee and then me." I said, "Sounds good to me." Deb said, "Okay."

We all opened up our air and checked our regulators then put on our wet, cold, wetsuits along with our dive gear. We started getting hot. We walked to the steps, went down them and then over close to the water. David said, "Don't forget to air up your BC's." We all aired them up.

David said, "Lee, tell us when." I said, "Okay." and started watching the waves. A big wave came in then another one. I said, "Now." We all hurried up, got in the water, put our fins on and started kicking out. I said to Deb, "Hurry,

Hurry, Hurry" and grabbed her air valve and started pulling her. We made it out past where the waves were breaking.

We slowed down and kicked over close to the reef. Deb said, "I'm ready." David and I said we were too. We put our masks on, our regulators in our mouths and got close together. We started letting the air out of our BC's. We got on the bottom and gave each other the okay signal.

Deb started going along looking at the reef. I was looking at the reef not too far from where Deb was. David was behind me. We were slowly going along. Deb was carefully looking at everything. Not missing even one little thing. David and I were looking too, just not as close as Deb was. We kept looking closely at it gradually getting deeper and deeper.

I checked my air. I was down to fifteen hundred pounds. We were at forty feet. I signaled to David and Deb for us to turn around and start back in. They gave me the okay signal. We turned around and started slowly going in, still looking at the reef. The surge started getting worse. I pointed up. Deb and David gave me the okay signal.

We went up. When we were on the surface, we aired up our BC's, took our regulators out of our mouths and our mask off. Deb said, "That's so neat there's so much life down there."

We slowly kicked in close to where the waves are breaking and started watching them. A big one went past us, then another. I said, "Now!" We all started kicking in fast. Some smaller waves were breaking and pushing us in. We could touch. We took our fins off and got out of the water.

Deb looked at me and said, "Here" and dumped her weights on the sand in front of me and said, "I'll never make it with them." David said, "Deb let me have your mask and fins." She handed them to him. We walked to the steps and started up them. Starting and stopping all the way up. We finally made it up the steps and to the car. We took our dive gear and wetsuits off. We loaded everything into the car. We were on our way to Deb's house.

Deb said, "When are we going diving again?" David said, "I can't go until next weekend." I said, "I'm going to Catalina on Monday but I can go any other day." Deb said to me, "I'm off on Thursday. Let's go then." I said, "Okay." Deb said to David, "Can I borrow your dive gear Thursday." David said, "Sure. You can borrow it anytime you need it."

We drove up to Deb's house. She unloaded her dive gear then David and I drove to his house. He unloaded his dive gear then I drove home, unloaded mine, rinsed it off and put it up.

Sunday …

I called Deb and asked her if she wanted to go to the dive shop. Deb said, "Yeah, pick me up. I need to take my dive gear back anyway." I loaded both mine and David's tanks in the car then drove to Deb's house and picked her up. We drove to the dive shop. I carried the tanks in and put them down at the filling area. Deb carried in her dive gear. Eddie was already filling some tanks. I said, "Man, it's busy for it being a Sunday!" Eddie said, "We're usually not open on Sunday's but since we're going to Catalina tomorrow, we opened for a few hours." I said, "Oh good. We lucked out then. I didn't know the dive shop was closed on Sunday's."

Eddie started filling the tanks and said, "Would you like to buy a dive card?" I said, "Yeah." Eddie finished filling the tanks then filled out a card for me, marking off four tanks. I said, "Thanks Eddie! I'll see you tomorrow." Deb and I loaded the tanks in the car. I took Deb home then I drove home and unloaded my tanks. I drove to David's and carried in his tanks. I talked to both David and mom for awhile then I went home.

Monday morning …

I got up and loaded my dive gear in the car. I went into the kitchen and took some medicine to prevent motion sickness. I get seasick real easy, especially when the boat stops and it starts rocking. I was ready to go.

I got in the car, drove to the donut shop, had a donut and a cup of coffee then drove to the boat docks. I found a good parking spot and parked. I unloaded my dive gear then picked it up and started walking.

I can see the boat. It looks like Ron is on it talking to some people. I walked down the dock to the boat. Ron said, "Put your tank over there with those tanks then find a place to strap your dive bag down with those dive bags." He was pointing at some tanks and dive bags then he said, "Put your weights on the floor under your dive bag. Then you'll need to sign in." I said, "Okay" and started putting everything up. I walked over to a table where a guy was talking to Debbie and filling out some paperwork. I got in line behind her.

He finished with Debbie then said to me, "Your dive card please." I got it out and handed it to him. He wrote down my name then handed it back to me and said, "Thank you." I stepped out of the way. I could smell bacon and eggs cooking, it smelled so good. A lot of divers were sitting and eating. I knew I would regret it if I ate anything like that. I got off the boat to go over to a drinking fountain that I saw near a building and took some more medicine for motion sickness. I got back on the boat and was ready to go.

The engines of the boat started. The deck hand untied the boat from the dock. We were on our way to Catalina. It was a nice, sunny, hot day. We went out through the breakwater. The waves were up so the boat was rocking back and forth fairly hard. I heard someone say, "I bet I shouldn't have eaten so much breakfast." I was glad I took motion sickness medicine!

I walked up to the front of the boat and looked at the waves. They didn't look like they were going to be very bad. I walked to the back of the boat and sat down. A lady walked up to me and said, "Do you know who I am?" I said, "I know you! You're Anita." Anita is Deb's friend. They went to school together. She sat down and we started talking.

Anita said, "I just got certified." I said, "I did too. How do you like it?" Anita said, "I really like it." I said, "I do too. I had to find a hobby after my divorce. It almost drove me crazy. Deb talked me into diving. We both got certified. She really likes it too." Anita said, "Oh that's too bad about you getting divorced. Don't you have kids?" I said, "Yeah, three." Anita said, "Isn't your oldest one a girl." I said, "Yeah the oldest is Mellissa, then Melinda then Lee Jr. I talked to my lawyer about fighting for them but he said he'll end up rich, I'll end up poor and she'll end up with the kids. Like I have enough money to make him rich. He said he has seen this before. He told me that I should just get a place to live, sit tight and they'll probably want to come live with me." Anita said, "I hope everything turns out okay." I said, "I hope so too. It's funny for some reason after we got divorced she went and got some tattoo's." Anita gave me a funny look. We kept talking for awhile then she walked back over to her friend and sat down.

After awhile I walked over to Ron. Ron said, "You, Debbie, Bob and I will be doing a deep dive for our first dive. I know you've met Debbie. Have you met Bob?" I said, "Nice to meet you Bob." Ron said, "Bob likes deep dives too. I want to try to do three dives on this trip. Usually we only have time for two so let's be ready and as soon as the boat anchors we'll go." We all said okay then Bob said, "Ron can lead and I'll be the last one." Debbie and I said okay.

Jim was sitting down a little way from Ron. Both Ron and Jim own the dive shop. Jim was working on some dive gear. He had his BC next to him. His wetsuit was strapped inside of his BC and he didn't have a dive bag. I said to Jim, "Where are your regulators at?" Jim said, "I put the top part of my wetsuit inside my BC. Then I put my regulators, hood, gloves, booties, and everything else I need on it. Then I put the bottom part of my wetsuit over everything and strap the BC straps around everything to hold it all together. That way it's easy to keep up with and easy to carry." I said, "Man, that's a good idea. I'm going to start doing that."

Ron walked up to me and said, "We'll be at the dive sight in a few minutes. Put your dive gear together but don't put your wetsuit on. We'll put them on when we get a little closer so we won't overheat." I said, "Okay."

I walked to my dive gear and started putting it together. After I got it all together, Ron said, "Okay we're pretty close. Let's put on our wetsuits and dive gear. After the boat stops, they will drop the anchor and we'll get in the water. We'll meet at the front of the boat at the anchor line." I said, "Okay" and started putting my wetsuit on. The boat slowed down and stopped. I heard them dropping the anchor.

Everyone on the boat was moving around, putting on their wetsuits and dive gear. The captain said over the intercom, "Okay, we're here! It's very deep here. Be extra careful. You can get well over a hundred feet easy. So everyone remember to be real careful and have fun."

I put my dive gear on and looked over at Debbie. She had her wetsuit on and was putting on her dive gear. I walked over to see if she needed any help. Anita was standing behind Debbie. Anita was wearing her bathing suit and putting on her wetsuit. I noticed she had some tattoos. I felt like a complete idiot!

Debbie was ready. We walked over to the side of the boat where a small hinged door was open. That's where we go in at. Eddie was standing next to the door holding onto us, to keep us steady and to keep us from falling as we're getting ready to step off. I looked down at the water. It's about four or five feet down. Eddie said, "Air up your BC. Get close to the edge and put your fins on then hold your regulator in your mouth with your left hand and your mask on with your right hand. Then just step off." I said, "Okay" and aired up my BC then stood in the opening and put my fins on. I put my mask on and my regulator in my mouth and held onto them.

I was nervous. Eddie was holding on to me. I looked down at the water. It looked like it was a long way down. I looked straight out over the water then stepped off. I splashed in the water and didn't move. I went down a couple of feet. Bubbles were all around me. I started floating up to the surface. What a relief! That was easy after all! I kicked out of the way and took my regulator out of my mouth.

Debbie was next. She stepped off and splashed in the water then floated back up. We kicked up to the front of the boat. We held onto the anchor line and waited for Ron. We saw Bob go in, then Ron. They kicked over to us. Ron said, "Our dive plan is to go to a hundred feet then start back up or if anyone gets down to fifteen hundred pounds of air we'll turn around and start back up." We all said okay. Ron said, "Let's go down the anchor line and meet on the bottom."

Ron put his regulator in his mouth, started letting air out of his BC and started going down. I put my regulator in my mouth and started letting the air out of my BC. I started going down the anchor line hand over hand. I was having a little trouble holding onto the anchor line and using both of my hands to pop my ears, but I was doing it. I could already tell this was going to be fun. The water was blue and crystal clear.

I could see Ron below me, down the anchor line about twenty feet. I was looking out, then down, then up at the boat. It looked really weird looking up at the bottom of the boat. The bottom of the boat just looked like some painted boards and it really didn't look like it was in that good of shape! Above the water, it was in real good condition. I kept looking around as I was getting deeper and deeper. I couldn't believe how neat it was to be in such clear water! It seemed as though I could see everywhere! I kept going down.

I was on the bottom with Ron not far from the anchor. We looked up at Debbie and Bob. They had about ten more feet to come down.

We're all on the bottom. Ron gave each one of us the okay hand signal. We all gave it back. I looked at my computer. We were at seventy feet. I thought this is neat being down this deep! Ron waved at us and started going along the bottom. I started following him. I looked back at Debbie. Bob was right behind her. I started noticing that we were going down the side of a hill, as if we were walking down a trail around a mountain. It was deeper to my right and shallower to my left.

We kept going down, around the hill, getting deeper and deeper. We were at ninety feet. We kept going.

We were at a hundred feet. I looked back at Debbie and Bob then looked back at Ron. Ron was moving away from me fast. I looked at where he was headed. It was a weight belt sitting on the bottom. Ron grabbed it then pointed for us to head back toward the boat. We all gave him the okay signal and started following him.

We went back up the side of the hill then straight over to the anchor. Ron gave me the signal to go up first. I started up. I was about half way up and looked down the anchor line and saw Debbie, then Bob, with Ron being last. I stopped at fifteen feet for our safety stop.

Everyone came up next to me and stopped. Ron had the weight belt over his shoulder but I could tell he was tired of holding it. After a few minutes, we went up to the surface. Bob quickly kicked to the back of the boat and got out. Ron started kicking toward the back of the boat. Debbie and I stayed close to him.

Ron handed Bob the weight belt and said, "I hate to think about why this was down there."

We all took our fins off and climbed up onto the boat. We took our dive gear off. Ron said, "Okay! Let's disconnect our regulators from our tanks and get our tanks aired up. We want to be ready to get in as soon as we stop at the next dive location. We'll try to do two dives there." Debbie, Bob and I said okay. Ron said, "Lee and Debbie, you're now certified deep divers." I said, "Good! Thanks Ron." We carried our tanks over to the filling area. The deck hand walked over and filled them. We took our wetsuits off and dried off.

The other divers started coming back in. The captain started cooking hamburgers and chicken on the grill. The grill is mounted on the back corner of the boat. It smelled really good and I was starving! I thought I don't feel seasick at all so I'm going to try it. I walked over to the captain and asked if I could have a hamburger. The captain said "Give me about a minute. There are chips and sodas too! Just help yourself." I said, "Okay, thanks."

I walked over to the cooler and got a soda, grabbed a bag of chips then walked back over to the captain. He handed me a hamburger. I sat down and ate it. It was really good. I started talking to some other divers.

The captain was going back and forth putting chicken and hamburgers on the grill and buns on paper plates. People would walk up and he would hand them a plate. I heard some yelling and looked over just in time to see a seagull swoop down and get a hamburger off the grill! As the seagull was flying off it would drop the hamburger in the air, then catch it again. You could tell it was hot and hard to keep in its mouth!

After a while the captain said, "Last call for hamburgers and chicken." Ron walked over to his dive gear and picked up a piece of paper then started counting people. Ron said, "It looks like everyone is back but we need to take roll just to make sure." Ron started reading off everyone's name. We all said, "Here!"

The captain started the engines and the deck hand started pulling up the anchor. I walked to the front of the boat to watch. He finished pulling it up. We were on our way to the next dive location.

We were all sitting around, just talking. Ron said to Debbie, Bob and I, "Okay when we stop, be ready to go. We don't want to waste any time or we won't have time for two dives." We all said okay.

After awhile Ron said, "We're almost there. Make sure your dive gear is ready. I'll let you know when to put your wetsuits on." We got up and checked our dive gear.

After a few minutes Ron gave us the okay signal. We put our wetsuits on then Ron gave us the okay signal and pointed at our dive gear. We put our dive gear on. The captain slowed the boat down. Everyone started putting their wetsuits on. The deck hand dropped the anchor, the captain shut off the engines while saying over the intercom, "Okay folks, we're here. It's not as deep here but you still need to be careful."

We weren't very far from shore this time and there was kelp everywhere. It was floating on the surface and we could see it underwater. Ron said, "Get in and meet at the anchor line." Debbie and I walked over to the opening where we were to go in at. Eddie walked up and said, "Boy, you guys aren't messing around." Eddie started holding onto me. I aired up my BC then stood in the opening and put my fins on. Then put my mask on and my regulator in my mouth and held onto them. I looked down at the water and all the kelp then straight out over it. I stepped off and splashed in the water. I didn't move. I went down a couple of feet then floated up to the surface. It was really easy this time. I kicked out of the way and took my regulator out of my mouth. Debbie stepped off and splashed in the water then floated back up. We started kicking toward the front of the boat then heard a splash. It was Bob. Then we heard another splash. It was Ron.

We were all at the anchor line. Ron said, "Okay our dive plan is to just stay together and start back in when anyone gets down to fifteen hundred pounds. Follow me, just like you did on the last dive. Let's go down the anchor line and meet on the bottom."

Ron put his regulator in his mouth and started letting air out of his BC and started going down. I put my regulator in my mouth and started letting the air out of my BC. I started going down the anchor line hand over hand. It sure was awkward holding the anchor line and popping my ears so I started to quickly let go of the anchor line, pop them, and grab a hold of the anchor line again. That was a lot better. I was about half way down and I could see Ron already on bottom looking up waiting on us. I looked around and couldn't get over how clean and clear the water was.

I got down to the bottom and went over next to Ron. We were forty feet deep. The bottom had big boulders everywhere. There was kelp from the bottom all the way to the surface and laying on the surface too. Everyone got to the bottom. Ron gave everyone the okay hand signal. We gave it back.

Ron started going along the bottom. I was right behind him, then Debbie and finally, Bob. Ron was going up and over, around the big boulders and through the kelp. All of a sudden Ron sped up, turned around and grabbed this big piece of kelp that was laying on the bottom. He started pulling on it. It was like he was pulling a tablecloth off of a table. He pulled it and sitting still on the bottom under the kelp was a four-foot shark about ten feet from me, pointed straight at me! I thought oh crap! It was just sitting there not moving. I wasn't moving either. I kept staring at it. It slowly swam a little toward me then turned right and started swimming off. It went a little way, then stopped and went back down to the bottom. It was like, "*Leave me alone.*" We all looked at it for a couple of minutes. Then Ron waved for us to start going.

We all started going again. We were at fifty-four feet and my pressure was down to fifteen hundred pounds. I kicked up next to Ron and pointed at my pressure gauge. Ron gave me the okay signal then turned around and headed back toward the anchor. We were going up, over the boulders and through the kelp.

We could see the anchor line. We went over to it. Ron started up. He was looking at his computer and going hand over hand up the anchor line. I was going up right behind him. Ron stopped for the safety stop at fifteen feet. Debbie, Bob and I went up next to him.

I looked at Ron and put my hand wide open on top of my head, sort of like a shark fin, with my eyes wide open like they were going to pop out of my head. I could tell Ron thought that was funny. He knew I was excited about that shark.

We went to the surface, aired up our BC's, took our masks off and our regulators out of our mouths. I said, "What kind of shark was that?" Ron said, "A horn shark. They're docile sharks." I said, "I thought you said it's rare to see a shark." Ron said, "It's rare to see a dangerous shark. You see sharks like those pretty often." I said, "I thought all sharks that big were dangerous. When I saw you pulling at that kelp, I was wondering what you were doing. Then when I saw the shark, I couldn't believe it." Ron started laughing and remarked, "That was a fun dive."

We kicked to the back of the boat and got out. Ron said, "Leave your wetsuit on, get your tank aired up and we'll do a short surface interval before we do another quick dive." We all disconnected our regulators from our tanks and carried them to filling area. The deck hand came over and filled them up. A few minutes later Ron said, "Let's get ready and meet at the anchor line."

I put my dive gear back on then went over to help Debbie with hers. We walked over to the opening where we go in. We were by ourselves, no Eddie this time. I said, "Eddie must be diving." Debbie said, "Yeah, he must be." I said, "I'll hold onto you while you put your fins on." She put her fins on then I said, "I can put my fins on by myself, go ahead and I'll meet you in the water." Debbie aired up her BC then put her mask on and her regulator in her mouth and stepped off.

She splashed in the water, then floated back up and moved out of the way. I put my fins on, aired up my BC, put my mask on and my regulator in my mouth, then stepped off. I splashed in the water and went down a couple of feet. I heard a splash and then another splash right next to me. I floated up to the surface then Ron and Bob floated up next to me. We all took our regulators out of our mouths and kicked up to the anchor line.

Ron said, "Our dive plan is to stay together and stay less than forty feet. Let me know when anyone gets down to fifteen hundred pounds." Then Ron grabbed his regulator and said, "Follow me" and put his regulator in his mouth and started dumping the air out of his BC.

I put my regulator back in my mouth, started letting the air out of my BC and started going down, popping my ears on the way. I can see Ron. He was almost on the bottom already. I kept watching him. He got down to the bottom and didn't stop. He just kept on going. I was thinking, "Oh crap! I had better hurry up!" I quickly started going down.

I got down to the bottom and took off toward Ron. I can barely see him going through the kelp. He went over to some really thick kelp and stopped. I caught up to him and got next to him. We turned around and waited for Debbie and Bob. Ron gave everyone the okay hand signal. We all gave it back.

Ron turned around and took off really quick into the thick kelp. I stayed right behind him, only a foot or two from his fins. Ron was going fast through the kelp, then he would turn one way and then the other. We were like rats going through a maze. I knew if I didn't stay really close to him he would lose me, so I kicked and turned, staying right behind him.

All of a sudden Ron started pulling away from me. Debbie and Bob went flying past me. I was kicking hard and not going anywhere. I looked down at my fins. There's one little strand of kelp about as big around as a pencil that was between the buckle on my fin and my fin. I reached down and pulled it out.

I can go now but I don't know where anyone is. I stayed still and looked around for them. After a little bit I saw someone. It was just a glance in between the kelp but they were about ten feet away. I quickly kicked in that direction. It's Bob. I kicked over behind him and started following him.

Everyone was going a little slower now, but not much. I followed Bob around some thick kelp, then we turned sharp to the left and my fins came out of the water. I looked up. I was only about two feet below the surface! I looked down at the bottom. It was only about ten feet deep. I tried to dump more air out of my BC but there wasn't any in it.

I checked my air. I was down to fifteen hundred pounds. I quickly kicked up next to Ron and gave him the hand signal of ten fingers, then five fingers. Ron pointed for us to go up. We all went up to the surface, aired up our BC's and took our regulators out of our mouths. I said, "I'm down to fifteen hundred pounds." Ron looked at Debbie and said, "How much air do you have?" Debbie said, "Nineteen hundred." Bob said, "I've got twenty one hundred." Ron said to Debbie and Bob, "You guys want to keep diving?" They both said yes. Ron said to me, "Do you think you can make it back to the boat on your own?" I looked over at the boat. It looked like it was a long way away. I said, "Sure." Ron said, "You'll probably want to go down about five feet to get under this kelp canopy. If you try going through it on the surface it's really hard. We'll meet you on the boat." I said, "Okay."

I looked back at the boat and set my compass heading marker toward the center of the boat. I put my regulator back in my mouth and let the air out of my BC. I went down about five feet or so just under the kelp canopy. I was holding my compass in front of my face where I could always see it. I went as straight as I could, going around the kelp trying to stay on course. I checked my air I'm down to nine hundred pounds. I went up to the surface. I'm only about fifty feet from the boat.

I checked my compass heading, went back down and started going again. I can see the bottom of the boat. I went up to it, went under it and started looking at the bottom of it. I was headed toward the back. I looked at the two propellers and two rudders. I was about five feet from them. I didn't want to get too close to them. I thought if I go up at the back or the side of the boat and someone jumps in the water they might land on me, so I turned around and went back up to the front of the boat. I went up to the surface and aired up my BC. I kicked to the back of the boat, climbed up on it and walked over to my dive bag. The boat was full of divers. They were sitting around having drinks and talking about the dives. I started taking my dive gear and wetsuit off then looked over at the back of the boat and saw Ron, Bob and Debbie getting out. I packed up all my dive gear the same way Jim packed his and put it up.

Ron took his dive gear off and said, "Okay, let's take roll." He called out everyone's name. We all said, "Here." The captain started the engines and the deck hand started pulling up the anchor. I went to the front and watched. There was a lot of kelp on the anchor line as he was pulling it in. He had a machete and was chopping it off as he was pulling up the anchor.

We were on our way back to the mainland. We all sat around talking about how much fun we had while having our drinks. We went through the breakwater and pulled up to the docks.

Ron thanked everyone for coming and said that he hoped we had fun. They tied the boat up to the dock. I waved at Ron and told him thanks. I grabbed all of my dive gear, walked to the car and drove home. I rinsed off my dive gear and put it away once I was home.

I walked into the house, called Deb and said, "I'm back from Catalina. You're going to have to go next time. It is so much better than beach diving. One step and your in the water. Visibility is perfect and the water is blue, not green. You're never going to guess who else went." Deb said, "Who." I said, "Anita. She said she just got certified too." Deb said, "I'll have to call her. I haven't talked to her for awhile." I said, "It was so much fun." Deb said, "I wish I could have gone."

Tuesday …

I called Deb and said, "I'm going to the dive shop to get air. Do you want to go?" Deb said, "Yeah. Come and pick me up." I loaded my tank, drove over and picked her up.

We drove to the dive shop and walked in. I put the tank at the filling area. We walked to the front. Eddie was behind the counter and said to me, "What did you think of Catalina." I said, "I really liked it. I'm ready to go again." Eddie said, "I know I like it too. It's my favorite place to dive." Deb said, "I wish I could have gone." Eddie said, "Are you guys going on the night dive with us on Saturday night?" I said, "That sounds scary but it sounds like fun. Where do you go night diving at?" Eddie said, "Shaw's Cove." Deb and I said, "Yeah we want to go." Eddie said, "You'll need to bring a chemstick and you should have two dive lights, a main one and a backup." I said, "What's a chemstick." Eddie said, "It's those green glowing sticks that the kids use at Halloween so they can be seen and won't get run over by a car." I said, "Oh yeah! I know what those are." Eddie said, "Everyone will have one so we can see each other."

Deb and I started looking at the dive lights. Eddie asked, "Do you have tanks to fill?" I said, "Yeah but only one." Eddie walked to the back and started filling it. Deb picked up a dive light and said, "I like this one." I was looking at one just like it and said, "I do too. It's not too big and not too small." It was about the size of a regular flashlight.

Eddie walked up and said, "That's the same size that I use but I also have one of these for my backup" he was pointing at a small one about half as big. Deb asked, "Do they work well?" Eddie said, "Yeah I never have any trouble with mine." Deb said, "I'll take one of each." I said, "I will too."

Deb and I paid for them, thanked Eddie and walked to the filling area. I grabbed my tank and carried it out to the car. I drove Deb home and then I went home.

I called David and said, "Deb and I are going with the dive shop on a night dive Saturday night. Do you want to go?" David said, "Yeah I'll go with you guys. I like night diving." I said, "Okay. We just bought our dive lights." David said, "I'll get mine out and check the batteries. Why don't you guys go with the dive shop and then I will go with you on the next dive." I said, "Sounds good to me."

Wednesday …

Deb called and left me a message saying that she borrowed David's dive gear and that she wanted me to call her tomorrow after I was ready.

Thursday …

I packed my dive gear, like Jim did on the Catalina trip. Everything was all packed nice and neat in my BC. It was so easy to carry now. I called Deb and asked her if she was ready. Deb said, "Yeah come pick me up." I said, "I'm on my way." I loaded my dive gear in the car and went and picked her up.

We were on our way to Shaw's Cove. Deb said, "I hope the waves are small." I said, "Me too." We were driving along and could see the water. Deb said, "Oh good! They look small." I said, "Good."

We drove up and parked, then got out and walked down the steps to where we could see the waves. Deb said, "Yeah. They're perfect! They're small!" I said, "Good." We walked back to the car and unloaded the dive gear. Deb said, "I hope I don't have any trouble with David's dive gear." I said, "He didn't have any trouble with it when we went diving. He said it worked good."

Deb was looking at David's BC and said, "What's this rope for?" I started laughing and said, "He mentioned tying a rope on his dump valve to let the air out of his BC instead of using his power inflator. He thinks it'll be easier that way." Deb said, "Oh gosh! Leave it to David to have ropes on his dive gear!"

We put our dive gear together, opened the air up and checked our regulators. I asked, "Are you ready to put your wetsuit on?" Deb said, "Yeah, but hurry up it's already getting hot!" I said, "Okay! I'll hurry." We put our wetsuits on then put our dive gear on.

We walked down the steps, then across the beach. We aired up our BC's, got in the water and put our fins on. Deb said, "This is nice when the waves are small." I said, "Yeah it's nice and peaceful." Deb asked, "What's our dive plan?" I said, "Lets turn around at fifteen hundred pounds." Deb said, "Okay." I said, "I'll follow you."

We kicked over close to the reef. Deb asked if I was ready. I told her that I was. We put our mask on, our regulators in our mouths and got close together then started letting the air out of our BC's.

We started slowly going down, popping our ears along the way. We were on the bottom. We were ten feet deep in the sand right next to the reef. We gave each other the okay signal. The visibility was good - about twenty feet.

Deb started going along the reef, close to the bottom. We were going real slow, looking at everything on the reef really good. We were at forty feet.

Deb kept looking at the reef. I turned, moving away from her and the reef about seven or eight feet. I turned upside down with my feet toward the surface and my head toward the sand. My buoyancy was perfect. I was floating upside down with my head about five feet off the bottom! I crossed my arms and put them against my stomach. I stayed still waiting for Deb to look at me.

After a few seconds she finally looked over at me. I could tell by the look on her face that she thought I was going crazy! I waved at her while I was upside down. She kept looking at me giving me a strange look. I turned upright then kicked over close to her.

We kept going along the reef. Deb stopped, quickly turned around and looked at me then pointed in front of us about five feet up ahead. I couldn't see anything. Deb looked at me and pointed like she was saying look, look! It was an octopus that was blended into the reef perfectly. Its head was bigger then a soda can. It was really neat looking and just sat there looking at us.

Deb slowly went toward it. She got about half way to it and it took off and went about ten feet further and higher on the reef. We kept looking at it then started going along the reef under it. I turned and went up the reef toward it. It took off away from us and went out of sight.

We kept going out, looking at the reef. Deb started pointing up ahead again. I looked where she was pointing. It was some big starfish. We went up to them and started looking at them. They are big, white starfish all together in one area. There must be thirty or forty of them. They looked neat but they looked strange because they were all so close together. We slowly went past them and kept looking at the reef.

I was down to fifteen hundred pounds. I signaled to Deb for us to turn around and start back in. She gave me the okay signal.

We turned around and started in. We went past the starfish. We kept going slow, looking at the reef. We were at twenty-five feet and my air was down to seven hundred pounds so I signaled to Deb to go up. She gave me the okay signal.

We got close together and started up. We were dumping air out of our BC's as we were going up. We got on the surface, aired up our BC's, took our regulators out of our mouths and our mask off. Deb said, "That octopus and those starfish were really neat." I said, "Yeah they were." Deb asked, "What were you doing upside down?" I said, "The way you can balance yourself in the water and how it feels like you're a bird flying around is neat!" Deb said, "I thought you were flipping out!"

We floated around and rested then I said, "Are you ready to get out?" Deb said, "Yeah but I'm not ready to walk up the steps!" We kicked in close, took our fins off and got out. Deb said, "Here, take my weights." I said, "Here. Give me your fins and mask too." She handed them to me. We walked across the beach and started up the steps. Deb stopped and rested like usual then took off. We made it to the top of the steps then over to the car. We took our dive gear and wetsuits off. We changed tanks and rested.

After awhile I asked, "Are you about ready for our next one?" Deb said, "I'm ready." We opened our air up and checked our regulators. We put our wetsuits and dive gear on. Deb said, "Let's go before we get hot." I said, "Let's go." We walked to the steps and down them, then across the beach. Deb said, "Let's get in." I said, "Okay." We aired up our BC's and got in.

We put our fins on then kicked over close to the reef. I said, "I'll follow you." Deb said, "Okay." We put our mask on, our regulators in our mouths, got close together and started letting the air out of our BC's. We started slowly going down, popping our ears on the way.

We were on the bottom close to the reef. We gave each other the okay signal. Deb started going along the reef. I was following her. We were looking close at the different types of plants and fish. The fish were swimming right up to us only a foot or two away, especially the big, orange, garibaldi's.

We kept going out looking in the cracks and holes in the reef. We started getting close to the group of big, white starfish again. I started watching Deb. She kicked up to them. She started touching one then started pulling up one of its arms. She carefully peeled the starfish off the reef and turned it upside down. She was holding it in her hands looking at the bottom of it. It was big! She turned it over back and forth looking at it really close. She looked over at me and gave me this look like this is the greatest thing in the world.

She took it and put it over her head. Like it was the halo on an angel. I thought surely she doesn't think she's an angel! She put it on the top of her head and let go of it. She looked weird. That starfish was so big that if it put its arms down over her head it would probably cover up her whole head, but it stayed stiff and flat while it was sitting up there.

She reached up, took it off her head and started putting it back down. She was being really careful not to hurt it. She carefully put it back exactly where she got it from. We started going out again looking at the reef. I checked my air. I was down to fifteen hundred pounds. I signaled to Deb to turn around and start back in. She gave me the okay signal.

We turned around and started in. We were going slow looking at the reef. We were at twenty-three feet and my air was down to six hundred pounds. I signaled to Deb to go up. She gave me the okay signal. We got close together and started up. We were dumping air out of our BC's on the way up.

We got on the surface, aired up our BC's, took our regulators out of our mouths and took our mask off. Deb said, "Those starfish are really neat and those garibaldi's seem so tame the way they come up to us. We should bring some fish food and feed them next time." I said, "That's a good idea that'll be fun feeding them."

We floated around and rested. Deb said, "It's so easy when you're underwater. You're weightless and it takes little effort to move around. Then, when you get out everything is heavy, it's hard to move and all clunky." I said, "I know. Isn't that funny. It's like going from one extreme to the other." Deb said, "I wish we could just stay down there." I said "Me too."

We kicked in close, took our fins off and got out. Deb handed me her weight belt, fins, mask and said, "I'm already worn out." We walked across the beach and started up the steps. Deb stopped and rested, as usual, then took off. We finally made it to the top of the steps and then over to the car.

We took our dive gear and wetsuits off. We loaded everything in the car. We were on our way to Deb's house. Deb asked, "We're going on our night dive Saturday night right?" I said, "Yeah. We need to get air." Deb said, "Yeah and chem-sticks." I said, "Let's go tomorrow." Deb said, "Okay."

I took Deb home. She unloaded her dive gear. I said, "If you want I'll keep David's tanks and rinse them off so you don't have to carry them." Deb said, "Sounds good to me." I went home and rinsed off the dive gear and put it up.

Friday …

I called Deb and said, “Ready?” Deb said, “Ready.” I loaded all four tanks in the car, drove to Deb’s house and picked her up. We drove to the dive shop and carried in the tanks. Eddie walked up and started filling them for us. He said, “Are you guys ready for Saturday night?” I said, “Yeah! It’s going to be scary.” Eddie said, “It’s not that bad.” Deb said, “It sounds like it’s going to be fun.” Eddie said, “It is.” Eddie finished filling the tanks. Deb and I loaded the tanks in the car, drove to my house and unloaded them. We drove to the department store, went in and found the chemsticks. Deb said, “Let’s get some extras.” I said, “Okay.” We paid for them then I drove Deb home and went home.

Chapter 3

Night diving

Saturday evening …

Deb called and said, "Scott is going with us. He wants to take the dogs so we'll go in the truck and meet you guys down there. Scott wants to know if you'll give me a ride home if the dogs cause any trouble and he has to leave." I said, "Yeah. That's no problem. David and I will meet you guys down there." Deb said, "Okay."

I called David and asked, "Are you about ready to go do a night dive?" David said, "I'm ready." I said, "I'm on my way." David said, "Okay."

I loaded my dive gear and the tanks in the car. I drove over and picked up David. We were on our way to Shaw's Cove. We drove by an area where we could see the ocean. David was looking at the waves and said, "They look small." I said, "Good."

We drove up close to the steps going to Shaw's Cove. It was crowded with divers. We kept driving until we found a parking spot down the street and parked. I said, "Man is it crowded."

Scott was walking toward us. He walked up to my window. I said, "Where did you guys park?" Scott said, "Over there on that little street" he was pointing at a little one way street. I grabbed two of the chemsticks then David and I got out of the car. We walked with Scott back to his truck. Deb was sitting in the cab. Scott let the dogs out to walk around with us behind the truck. We were talking and looking at all the divers. I opened up a chemstick and asked, "How do you light these things?" Deb said, "Bend it in the middle until it cracks." I bent it. It cracked and started glowing. Deb grabbed hers, cracked it, then tied it to her tank.

I looked around and saw Ron. He was unloading his dive gear behind his truck. I said, "Hey there's Ron. Let's go talk to him." Scott put the dogs in the back of the truck. We all walked over to Ron. Ron said, "We'll get in right before the sun goes down. So we'll need to be ready in about ten or fifteen minutes. We have a big group so we'll probably split up into two or three smaller groups. There must be a couple of other dive shops here too." I said, "Okay we'll be ready."

Deb and Scott walked back to the truck. David and I walked back to the car. When we got to the car I unloaded my dive gear, put it together and tied my chemstick to my tank. I put my wetsuit and dive gear on. David said, "I'm going to stay with Scott while you guys are down." I said, "Okay." David said, "There's Deb." I looked over at her. She was walking toward the steps. David said, "Go ahead. I'll lock the car." I said, "Okay" and walked over to Deb. Deb said, "Ray asked us to meet on the beach. We're going with him." I said, "Okay."

We walked down the steps and over to the middle of the beach. The beach was crowded. There were divers everywhere. The sun was just going down but there was still light so we could see. Ray walked up with four other divers and said, "This is our group – seven of us. Let's try to stay together. Let's get in and kick over close to the reef." We all said okay and started walking around the other divers.

We aired up our BC's, turned on our dive lights, got in the water and put our fins on. It was gradually getting darker. We kicked over close to the reef. There were divers everywhere, on the surface next to us and underwater beneath us. There were dive lights and chemsticks shining everywhere.

Ray said, "Okay, let's try to stay together. Is everyone ready?" We all said yes. Ray said, "Let's meet on the bottom." I thought man this is scary. I'm glad there's a lot of other divers here. We all put our mask on and our regulators in our mouths. We started letting the air out of our BC's. Deb and I were next to each other, inches apart. We were slowly going down popping our ears on the way. I looked around, divers, dive lights and chemsticks were everywhere. I wasn't sure which one was Ray or anyone for that matter, in our group. Deb and I went to the bottom, got on our knees and gave each other the okay signal.

We stayed still on the bottom and looked around for Ray or anyone from our group. I saw a diver and their fins had yellow markings on them like Ray's. I thought that must be him. I patted Deb on her arm and took off toward him. I grabbed his fin and held onto it. He turned around and looked at me. I waved at him. Wait! That's not Ray! I've never seen this guy before. I let go of his fin and waved at him. I looked at Deb, pointed to her, then myself and then toward the reef meaning let's go on our own. Deb gave me the okay signal. We started going on our own.

Deb was close to the reef and I was next to her on her left side. We were slowly going shining our dive lights on the reef while staying real close together. We kept going along close to the bottom, next to the reef. There were several divers in front of us and several behind us. We could see dive lights shining up, down, left and right all over the place (like a bunch of new night divers would be shining them). All the divers had chemsticks glowing that were tied onto their tanks. We could only see for about ten feet from the beam of our dive light. The other divers were stirring up the sand off the bottom, making it to where we can't see very far at all at times. We kept going slow looking at the reef on our right side then out toward the dark, flat, sandy, open ocean to our left side.

I kept shining my dive light out to the left but the beam would gradually dim to gray, then black darkness. I thought that's the open ocean out there, there are man-eating sharks out there and here we are out here at night. I told myself, look at the reef, look at the reef and don't think about it. I could feel my heart starting to beat faster and faster. I was getting really scared but none of the other divers seemed to be scared, not even Deb. I kept looking at the reef with Deb. We were shining our dive lights on it, looking at the small animals and plants.

I looked back out toward the open ocean. I could see a fish about a foot long sitting on the sandy bottom, looking like it was asleep. I looked back at the reef and told myself, quit looking out there. I was so nervous.

I checked my air. I was down to fifteen hundred pounds. We were at twenty-nine feet. I signaled to Deb that we needed to turn around and start back in. Deb gave me the okay signal. We turned around and started in. Deb stayed on the left side next to the reef. We kept looking at the reef while slowly going in. I kept trying to only look at the reef and to not think about the open ocean. The closer we were getting to the shore the calmer I was getting.

We were ten feet deep. I started having trouble staying on the bottom. I signaled to Deb to go up. She gave me the okay signal. We went up to the surface, aired up our BC's, took our regulators out of our mouths and our mask off. Deb said, "That was fun." I said, "Yeah it was but it sure was scary." Deb said, "Yeah, it was a little bit but not much." I looked around and said, "Man is it dark now." It was completely dark. We rested on the surface and kept our dive lights on. We floated around looking into the water next to the reef at all the divers shining their dive lights around.

I said, "Are you ready to get out?" Deb said she was. We kicked in close, took our fins off and got out. David was on the beach waiting for us. David said, "Scott took the dogs home." Then he grabbed Deb's weights, mask and fins. Deb said, "I was wondering how it was going to turn out with them." David said,

"How was it out there?" Deb said, "It's really neat. The fish are sleeping and it's more like creatures, instead of fish." David said, "Look at all the divers." I said, "I know it's really crowded. We even lost our group and went by ourselves."

We walked across the beach and started up the steps. Deb stopped and rested, as usual, then took off. We finally made it to the top of the steps and started walking toward the car. Ray was next to his truck taking his dive gear off. We walked over to him. I said, "We got separated as soon as we went down." Ray said, "Yeah, it was really crowded. Everyone just split up and went on their own." I said, "It was crowded."

We walked to the car and took our dive gear off. I left my wetsuit on. We started talking and resting. David looked at me and said, "I hope it's not this crowded when we go." I looked at him but didn't say anything.

Kate, the trainee instructor from the dive classes, walked past us with her dive gear on, going back to her car. We waved at her. She took her dive gear and wetsuit off then walked over to us. I said, "That was scary but it was fun." Kate said, "Yeah, I like doing night dives and I like diving at Shaw's." I said, "We do too. Do you want to go with us next time we go diving?" Kate said, "Sure that'll be fun." Deb said, "I can go Thursday." David said, "I can't go until Saturday." I asked Kate, "Can you go Thursday?" Kate said, "I'll only be able to do one dive in the morning." I said to Deb, "Is one dive okay?" Deb said, "Yeah, that's okay with me." I said, "Let's go Thursday then." Kate and Deb said okay. Kate said, "Where do you guys want me to meet you at?" Deb said, "Lee usually picks me up at my house. We can meet there if you want." Kate said, "Okay. I'll see you guys Thursday." Kate walked back to her car and drove away.

Divers were walking back to their cars, taking off their dive gear, packing everything up and leaving. There were hardly any cars around now. It was really dark and quiet. I changed my tank. David changed the tank that Deb used, then walked over to his dive bag and pulled out his dive light. I said, "Wow, that's a big dive light!" It was about as big as a car headlight. David said, "Yeah it is and it's been a good one." I said, "Are you about ready?" David said, "I'm ready when you are. Hopefully most of the divers have left." I was thinking how scary it would be if it *wasn't* crowded. David put his wetsuit on then we put our dive gear on. Deb said, "I'm going to stay in the car." I said, "Okay."

We walked over to the steps then started down them. As we were getting close to the beach, I started looking for divers on the beach or out in the water, looking for their dive lights or chemsticks. There weren't any, not even one. I couldn't believe it! Everyone had left! We started walking across the beach. David said, "Oh good. It looks like we're the only divers." There were a few people sitting on the beach watching the waves but we were the only divers. I took a big breath and said, "Yeah, we don't have to worry about the crowd on this dive." I started getting nervous.

David asked, "Are you ready get in?" I said, "Yeah." We turned our dive lights on, aired up our BC's, got in and put our fins on. We kicked over close to the reef. David asked, "Are you ready to go down?" I said, "I'm ready."

We got close together and started letting the air out of our BC's. We slowly went down to the bottom. We gave each other the okay signal. I looked at the beam from David's dive light. It was bigger and went further than mine. We started going, looking at the reef. I was next to the reef. David was on my left side next to the open ocean. I kept trying to only look at the reef and not even look out toward the open ocean. We were going fast, a lot faster than Deb and I went. It didn't seem as scary with David. I thought to myself he's experienced. He won't let anything happen to us.

We kept going fast looking at the reef, shining our dive lights up and down it. We weren't seeing much but with all the divers that were here earlier, I'm sure they scared everything off. I thought I'm glad we're not seeing anything! As we were getting deeper and deeper I would glance out toward the open ocean then quickly look back and tell myself not to look out there - there is nothing out there.

I checked my air. I was down to fourteen hundred pounds. We were fifty-three feet deep. I pointed at my pressure gauge then pointed in. David gave me the okay signal. We turned around. I got next to the reef. We started in, going fast and looking at the reef.

I checked my air. I was down to six hundred pounds. We were twenty-eight feet deep. I thought I don't want to go up and be on the surface out in the middle of the ocean at night. I started to panic, slightly. I could feel my breathing getting faster and deeper and my heart beating harder and harder. I grabbed David's arm and pointed with six fingers, then to my pressure gauge to let him know that I was down to six hundred pounds. I pointed in. David gave me the okay signal. We started going really fast.

We were looking, but not slowing down any. I was telling myself to breathe easy. I kept looking at my depth gauge twenty-two feet, eighteen feet, fourteen feet. I was down to three hundred pounds of air. I couldn't stay down. I was floating up really bad. I checked my BC. It didn't have any air in it.

I pointed up to David. He gave me the okay signal. We went up to the surface, aired up our BC's, took our regulators out of our mouths and our mask off. David said, "That was fun." I said, "It is, but scary." I looked toward the beach.

All I could see was a few lights on the houses. I said, "It sure is dark." David said, "Yeah, this is great."

We kicked in close, took our fins off and got out. We walked across the beach and up the steps then back to the car. Deb was sitting in the car. David said, "That was fun." Deb said, "I know. I like it at night." We took our dive gear and wetsuits off. We loaded everything in the car.

We drove to Deb's house. Deb unloaded her dive gear then David and I drove to David's house. I said, "I'll fill your tanks if you want me to." David said, "Okay." He unloaded his dive gear. I drove home, unloaded my dive gear, rinsed it off and put it up.

Tuesday …

I loaded the tanks in the car, drove to the dive shop, carried them in and put them at the filling area. I walked up to the front. Ron was working behind the counter. Ron said, "What do you think about night diving" and started walking toward the filling area. I said, "It was fun but it sure is scary." Ron started filling the tanks and said, "After you do it a few times, it's not as scary." I said, "Good. Deb and David really liked it." Ron finished filling the tanks. I said, "Thanks Ron." I loaded the tanks in the car and drove home.

Thursday …

I loaded my tanks and dive gear then called Deb. I said, "I'm on my way." Deb said, "Good. Kate just called and said she was too. I got us some fish food so that we can feed the fish." I said, "Good. That will be fun."

I drove up and parked behind Kate's car. We loaded all the dive gear into my car. We were on our way to Shaw's Cove. Deb said, "I hope the waves are small." Kate said, "Me too. I don't like it when the waves are big." Deb said, "I don't either. I brought some fish food this time so we can feed the fish." Kate said, "Have you ever fed the fish a sea urchin?" Deb responded no with her nose all scrunched up like it was gross. Kate said, "I'll show you how to do it."

We drove by an area where we could see the ocean. Deb looked at the waves and said, "Good, they looked small." Kate said, "Good." We drove up to Shaw's Cove and parked, close to the steps.

We unloaded the dive gear and put it together. We opened up our air and checked our regulators. Kate said, "What's our dive plan?" I said, "Why don't we just try to stay together and start back in when someone gets down to fifteen hundred pounds." Deb and Kate said okay. Kate said, "Lets all put our wetsuits on together or we'll get hot." Deb said, "I'm ready." I said, "Me too." We put our wetsuits on, then put our dive gear on. Deb lifted up a small bag and said, "I've got all the fish food in this bag. If anyone wants any just let me know and I'll give you some. I'm going to tuck it into my wetsuit." Kate and I said okay.

We walked to the steps and went down them then across the beach. I said, "Don't forget to air up your BC's. We aired them up. We got into the water and put our fins on. Deb said, "I like it when the waves are like this." Kate and I both agreed.

We kicked over close to the reef. Kate asked if we were ready. Deb and I both responded that we were. Kate said, "Let's meet on the bottom." Deb and I said, "Okay." We put our mask on and our regulators in our mouths. We got close together then started letting the air out of our BC's and popping our ears on the way down.

We were on the bottom. We got on our knees then gave each other the okay signal. We were twelve feet deep. The visibility was really good. Deb pulled the fish food bag out of her wetsuit. It was full of air and trying to float. She let the air out and let water go into the bag. Kate started waving at us to follow her. She started going along next to the reef. Deb followed her and I followed Deb.

We went out a little way looking at the reef. Fish were starting to come around us. Deb grabbed her fish food bag, opened it and started feeding a couple of fish next to her. Just a few seconds later there were fish all around her. Deb reached in her bag and gave Kate and I some fish food. We started feeding them too. Fish were everywhere! We kept feeding the fish.

Kate and I ran out of fish food. Deb put the bag back in her wetsuit, then held her hands open, up next to her shoulders with her finger tips pointing out showing us that she was out of fish food.

Kate started moving around. Deb and I looked over at her. She was doing something. She had her dive knife in her hand and went over to a rock that had some sea urchins on it. She pried one off the rock with her dive knife. Deb and I looked at each other then looked back at Kate. Kate looked at us and pointed at the sea urchin. She turned it upside down, stabbed it in the middle and cracked it in half, then held it up. The fish started swimming around it eating all the insides out of it. The only thing the fish left was the shell. I looked over at Deb. She looked like she was sick and completely disgusted. I was thinking about Deb being such an animal lover, that she doesn't even kill spiders, and I know she wouldn't ever kill a sea urchin.

Deb looked over at the reef. She went over to it and started looking at it. I went over next to Deb and started looking at it too. Then, Kate came over next to us. We started slowly going out looking at the reef.

I checked my air. I was down to fifteen hundred pounds. We were forty feet deep. I pointed at my pressure gauge and pointed in. Deb and Kate gave me the okay signal. We turned around and started back in. We kept on going slowly while looking at the reef.

We were ten feet deep. I started having trouble staying on the bottom. I signaled to Deb and Kate that I was going up. We all went up to the surface and aired up our BC's. I said, "If you guys have enough air you can go ahead and keep diving and I'll wait for you. I was having trouble staying down again." Deb and Kate said okay and went back down.

I kicked around on the surface looking down at them. After a few minutes they came back up. Deb said, "That was so neat feeding the fish the fish food but I won't ever feed them a sea urchin." Kate said, "I know it is mean." Deb said, "That was so neat having all those fish around us." Kate and I said, "It was."

We floated around and rested for awhile then Deb said, "I don't want to get out." Kate said, "I know getting out is the worst part." We floated around a little longer then I asked, "Are you guys ready to get out?" Deb and Kate said yes.

We kicked in close, took our fins off and got out. Deb handed me her weights, mask and fins. Kate looked at me and asked, "Do you want mine too?" I said, "I'll try." Kate said, "I was only joking." I said, "Watch Deb, she barely makes it back to the car." Kate nodded, acknowledging that she would.

We walked to the steps and started up them. Deb stopped all of a sudden, like usual, and rested. Kate and I stopped behind her and exchanged looks to each other. After a few seconds Deb took off up the steps. Kate and I stayed right behind her. We kept stopping behind Deb, then taking off with her, staying right behind her. We finally made it to the top of the steps then back to the car.

We took our dive gear and wetsuits off then packed everything in the car. We were on our way to Deb's house. We drove up and parked behind Kate's car. Deb and Kate unloaded their dive gear. Deb carried hers to the backyard. I helped Kate load hers into her car. Deb walked over to us and said, "I'm tired." Kate said, "Me too. I'm going home and resting. Thanks for letting me go with you guys." Deb and I said, "You're welcome." Kate drove off. I drove home, unloaded my dive gear, rinsed it off and put it up.

Friday …

I loaded the two empty tanks into the car and drove to the dive shop. I carried the tanks in and put them at the filling area. Eddie was putting up some dive gear. I asked, "Can I get some air when you get a chance?" Eddie said, "Sure" and walked over and started filling the tanks. I said, "Deb took some fish food with us yesterday. We had fish all around us." Eddie exclaimed, "That's neat isn't it?" I said, "Yeah, it is. Do you have any books that show pictures of the different types of fish?" Eddie said, "Yes we do. They are on the bookshelf in the front." I said, "Okay, thanks. I'm going to go take a look at them."

I walked up to the front and started looking at the books. I looked through a few and found one with a lot of pictures of fish and sea animals. I thought this is a good one! Eddie walked up. I said, "I think I like this one the best." Eddie said, "That's a good one." I said, "I'll take it and can I get four more pounds of weight. I always have trouble at the end of the dive. I start floating up even without any air in my BC." Eddie said, "That is what's bad about aluminum tanks, the lower your air gets the worse they float. So you have to carry extra weight." I said, "I'm finding that out. I also read in a magazine that the best way to weigh yourself is, be at fifteen feet with five hundred pounds of air, no air in your BC and *then* you should be neutral." Eddie said, "That sounds like a good way to weigh yourself." I said, "I know. I wonder why they don't weigh you like that when you take dive lessons?" Eddie said, "They like the students to be light when they're doing the classes." I said, "Oh, I guess that makes sense."

I carried the book and extra weights out to the car. Then loaded the tanks and went home. David called and said, "What do you think about night diving tomorrow night?" I said, "Okay but I've got to work nights tomorrow night so I'll probably only have time for one dive." David said, "Okay."

A little while later …

Deb called and said, "When are we going diving?" I said, "David and I are going tomorrow night. Do you want to go?" Deb said, "I can't but I can go Sunday. Let's do a night dive Sunday." I said, "Okay, but I'm working nights so I'll probably only have time for one dive." Deb said, "Okay."

Saturday evening …

David called and said he would be over in a little bit. I walked out to the garage and started getting ready. David drove up. I said, "I'll drive if you want." David said, "Okay." We loaded the tanks in the car. David got his dive gear and I got mine. We loaded our dive gear in the car.

We were on our way to Shaw's Cove. The sun had just gone down and it was dark. I said, "Deb brought some fish food and we fed the fish. It was really neat." David said, "I don't like to carry fish food on me because I don't want to be shark bait. I even heard of a diver that was spear fishing, he had bloody fish on a stringer that he tied to his waste. A shark came up and started eating the fish off the stringer." I said, "Oh you're kidding. That probably wasn't a very good idea. I didn't even think about something like that." David said, "The last thing I want to be is food." I said, "Me too."

We drove up to Shaw's Cove and parked. It was really dark. We unloaded the dive gear and put it together. We opened up our air, checked our regulators, cracked open our chemsticks and tied them to our tanks. David said, "You ready to put your wetsuit on?" I said, "Yeah, I'm ready." We put our wetsuits on then I walked over to David and helped him with his hood. We put our dive gear on then grabbed our fins, mask and dive lights. We started walking toward the steps. It was really dark now. I asked, "Is our dive plan going to be the same? To start back when one of us gets to fifteen hundred pounds?" David said, "Sounds good to me and I'll follow you." I said, "Okay."

We could hear the waves breaking but they sounded small. We walked down the steps then across the beach. There were some couples sitting on the beach but no divers were around. I said, "Man, I can't believe divers dive at night." David said, "It sure is fun. I don't know why divers dive in the daytime when they can dive at night."

We turned on our dive lights, aired up our BC's, got in the water and put our fins on. We kicked over to the reef. We were looking at the houses on the cliffs. David said, "The best way to know you're at the right cove when you are coming back in is to pick a light that you'll recognize. When you come back, you'll see it and hope it's not a porch light that someone turned off." I said, "That's a good idea" and started pointing at a light on the cliff and said, "What about that light over there?" David said, "That one will work. Are you ready to go down?" I said, "Yeah, I'm ready." We got close together and started letting the air out of our BC's. We were going down, popping our ears on the way down.

We were on the bottom. We were fifteen feet deep. We gave each other the okay signal. We could see about ten feet but only where our dive lights were shining. I started going along next to the reef. David was next to me, on my left side, the open ocean side.

We started going fast. We weren't slowing down or stopping at all. I was shining my dive light up and down on the reef then quickly over to David's side. David was shining his back and forth from his left side looking out to the open ocean then in front of me like a sweeping motion. I started doing it the same way, sweeping from the reef to out in front of David back and forth. We were going along fast and smooth. We could see really well by sweeping with our dive lights in this way.

I was feeling okay, just a little nervous, but nothing like before. We kept picking up speed, going faster and faster. We got to the opening where Deb went in to look at the fish. We kept going straight. I saw a shiny snail and shined my dive light on it back and forth. David shined his dive light on it. We stopped. We both looked at it for a few seconds then we started going again.

David was shining his dive light on something out in the sandy area. I shined mine out there on it too. It's a small fish on the bottom sleeping. I thought how weird seeing the fish sleeping. I checked my air I was down to fifteen hundred pounds. I signaled to David for us to turn around. He gave me the okay signal. We turned around and started back in.

I got next to the reef. David got back on the open ocean side. I didn't want to be on that side. We started going fast sweeping with our dive lights like before. I was staying just a couple of feet from the reef.

I started looking around. Something was wrong. The reef isn't looking right. It looks different for some reason, not like it did when we were going out. I thought what's going on? I check my air and our depth.

We slowed down and kept going. I checked my depth again. We were deeper now. I thought this can't be. We went a little further. We were getting deeper and deeper. I'm thinking how can we be getting deeper, something is wrong. I must be narced (nitrogen narcosis). The reef is on my left side, like we were going in but we're getting deeper. I signaled to David like what's going on. David slowly shook his head no. We went a little further both of us constantly watching our depth. We were getting deeper all right. David gave me the signal to turn around. I gave him the okay signal.

We turned around and slowly started going. We were getting shallower and shallower but the reef is on our right side. I'm thinking man, am I messed up. I checked our depth. We were at twenty-six feet. I checked my air. I'm down to five hundred pounds. I signaled to David to go up. He gave me the okay signal.

We got close together and started going up. We got on the surface, aired up our BC's, took our regulators out of our mouths and our mask off. I said, "What happened? That was weird." David said, "I don't know. We got turned around some how. Where's the light we saw before we went down?" I said, "They must have turned it off. I don't like being out this far and on the surface at night." David said, "Let's kick in."

We started kicking in. David said, "Let's turn our dive lights off so we won't be lit up so much." I said, "Okay." We both turned them off. It is really dark. David started looking around then turned his dive light back on and was looking at the cliffs. David said, "This doesn't look right. This isn't where we went in at."

I said, "You've got to be kidding." I turned my dive light on and started looking at the cliffs and said, "You're right. I've never seen this place before." We were shining our dive lights all around. I said, "I wonder where we're at?" David said, "We must have come into a different cove." I asked, "How could we have done that?" David said, "I don't know." I said, "I wonder if we need to go to the left or to the right." David said, "I'm not sure. Look there's some steps. Let's get out and go up and see if we recognize where we're at." I said, "Okay."

We kicked toward the steps. We can touch. We took our fins off and got out then walked up the steps to the street where they lead to. We started looking around. David said, "Why don't we walk around a little and try to figure out where we're at?" I said, "Okay."

We walked down the street to the next street. David said, "I think this is the street we parked on. I think we need to go that way." He started pointing down the street. I walked over and looked at the street sign at the corner and said, "It is." David said, "Good, the car can't be far. Let's walk and look for it." I said, "Okay."

We started walking. I started getting a rash from my wetsuit, my feet were getting sore and my back was starting to hurt from carrying my dive gear. I said, "I know how Deb feels now." We kept walking. David started pointing and said, "There it is." He was pointing at the car. I said, "Oh good, we've got to hurry or I'm going to be late for work."

We walked to the car. We quickly took our dive gear and wetsuits off. We crammed everything into the trunk. We were on our way to my house. I said, "What kind of snail was that? It had a shiny shell." David said, "A cowry. They have skin that wraps around the shell to protect it." I said, "Those are nice looking snails. Hey! Do you know what? I didn't have any trouble staying down this time. I think those four extra pounds are going to work out good." David said, "Good, are we going diving next Saturday night?" I said, "Sounds good to me."

We drove up to my house. I said, "If you want I'll fill the tanks." David said, "Okay." We got out and unloaded David's dive gear. I said, "Leave my dive gear in the car. I've got to go." David said, "You're going to wear your bathing suit to work?" I said, "Yeah. I'll change at work. I've got to go or I'll be late." David said, "Okay, I'll see you later."

Sunday evening …

I called Deb and asked if she was ready. She said she was. I told her I would be over in a few minutes. I drove over to Deb's house and picked her up. We were on our way to Shaw's Cove.

The sun was down. It was starting to get really dark. I said, "David and I got lost last night. We went out with the reef on our right side, like normal, then turned around and started back in. Some way we ended up going into the cove next to Shaw's Cove. I don't have any idea how we did it either. It was a really strange dive. I thought I was narced." Deb said, "I don't want to get lost. How deep did you go?" I said, "Around Sixty feet." Deb said, "Let's not go out that far. Let's not go out past fifty feet." I said, "Okay. I was so happy when we finally found the car. We walked all the way from that cove. It was a really long walk and I was almost late to work." Deb said, "Let's go down next to the reef, then set your compass and then go straight out until we're down to fifteen hundred pounds or out to fifty feet. Then, turn around and come straight back in." I said, "Okay."

We drove by the area where we can usually see the ocean. Deb said, "I couldn't see very good but I think the waves are small." I said, "They were pretty small last night." We drove to Shaw's Cove and parked. We could barely hear the waves. Deb said, "Good they sound small."

It was dark and quiet. We unloaded the dive gear, put it together, opened up our air and checked our regulators. We cracked open our chemsticks and put them on our tanks. Deb asked, "Are you ready to put your wetsuit on?" I said, "Yeah, I'm ready." We put our wetsuits on then our dive gear. We grabbed our fins, mask and dive lights, walked over to the steps and started down them. Deb said, "Boy this is different when it's not crowded." I said, "Yeah, it is different - a lot different."

We walked down the steps and across the beach. We aired up our BC's, turned on our dive lights, got in the water and put on our fins. We kicked over next to the reef. Deb said, "Don't let us get lost." I said, "I wouldn't do that. Are you ready?" Deb said she was.

We got close together, put our mask on, our regulators in our mouth and started letting the air out of our BC's. We were shining our dive lights straight down at the bottom. We were on the bottom and only eight feet deep.

We gave each other the okay signal. I pointed at the reef and went over real close to it. I looked down the reef and set my compass going straight out next to it. Deb came over next to me and looked at my compass. I gave her the okay signal. She gave it back.

Deb started going looking closely at the reef. I got beside her on the open ocean side. Every now and then I glanced out toward the open ocean. I kept telling myself nothing to worry about. Deb kept looking at the reef while going out, real slow. She was checking out every little nook and cranny while looking at all the small things. I would try not to think about the open ocean and try to only look at the reef. There were several cowries and other little creatures moving around on the reef. There wasn't any fish swimming around us at all. I glanced out toward the open ocean and saw a couple of fish sitting on the bottom, about seven or eight feet away from us. They looked like they were sleeping. I grabbed Deb's arm and showed her. We kicked over close to them and started looking at them. They looked really funny. We got a little closer. They woke up and quickly swam off.

We started kicking back toward the reef. Deb started waving at me and pointing at the sand. I looked where she was pointing. There was two eyes sticking out of the sand, looking at us. They were about the size of two small marbles. We could see the eyes moving around, watching us. We went over closer to them and started watching them. They were just eyes sticking out of the sand. We couldn't see any of its body. We looked at each other - like what in the world are these eyes doing out here? Deb poked it. It took off out of the sand and started swimming away. It was a flounder that had its eyes sticking up from the top of its head.

We went back over to the reef and kept going out while looking at it. I checked my air. I'm down to fifteen hundred pounds. We were at forty-six feet. I signaled to Deb for us to turn around. She gave me the okay signal. We turned around and started in.

Deb stayed on the reef side. I was holding my compass in my hand and staring at it. We kept going in, slow. Deb kept looking closely at everything on the reef. We were staying right on the double marker on the compass. We were getting shallower and shallower.

We were at fourteen feet. My pressure was down to five hundred pounds. I signaled to Deb for us to go up. She gave me the okay signal. We went up to the surface, aired up our BC's, took our regulators out of our mouths and our mask off. Deb said, "Man that is so neat. I didn't think I would like it that much at night but it's completely different down there at night." I said, "I know. It is pretty neat, but I get a little scared. I'm glad we didn't get lost. I really don't have any idea how we got lost." Deb said, "I don't either." I said, "I really don't like floating on the surface at night either." Deb said, "Oh you worry about everything." We started kicking in.

We kicked in to where we were able to touch. We took our fins off and got out. Deb handed me her weights, mask and fins. We walked across the beach and started up the steps. Deb said, "At least at night it's not hot." I said, "Yeah but it sure is dark." Deb did her usual stopping and starting all the way up the steps then we walked over to the car.

We took off our dive gear and wetsuits. We packed everything in the car. We were on our way to Deb's house. I said, "At least tonight I won't have to wear my bathing suit to work." Deb said, "You wear your bathing suit to work?" I said, "I had to last night. I was almost late." Deb said, "I can't believe you did that."

We drove up to Deb's house. She unloaded her dive gear. I drove home and unloaded my dive gear and quickly rinsed it off. I changed clothes then went to work.

Saturday evening …

I called David and asked if he was ready. He said he was. I loaded the tanks and my dive gear then drove to David's house. David loaded his dive gear. We were on our way to Shaw's Cove. The sun was down and it was dark. I said, "When I went and got air they said the surf was up. Hopefully it won't be too bad." David said, "Yeah, I would hate for us to drive all the way down there and not be able to dive." I said, "Me too. When Deb and I went last time I set my compass heading, we went straight out to forty six feet, turned around and came straight back in. We didn't get lost. I'm still not sure how we got lost and went over into the next cove." David said, "That was strange. Let's try to go straight out and straight back in." I said, "Okay."

We drove by an area not far from the ocean. David said, "I couldn't see very good but I think they're big." I said, "How big?" David said, "Big." We drove up to Shaw's Cove and parked. We could hear the waves crashing. They sounded big. I said, "Let's go look at them." We grabbed our dive lights and walked over to the steps and went down them to where we could see the waves. We turned on our dive lights, started shining them out at the waves and started watching them. They were big and the tide was real high. After the waves were breaking they were coming up almost all the way to the bottom of the steps. David looked at me and said, "What do you think?" I said, "We drove all the way down here to go diving. Let's go for it. The only thing that can happen is we get a little beat up. Let's just get out past the break then we should be okay." David said, "Okay, let's do it."

We walked back to the car, unloaded the dive gear and put it together. We put our wetsuits on. I helped David with his hood. We opened up our air and checked our regulators then put our dive gear on. David said, "Are you ready?" I said, "Yeah. I'm ready." We grabbed our fins, mask and dive lights and walked over to the steps. We were walking down the steps. I said, "I hope this turns out okay." David said, "Me too."

We got close to the bottom of the steps. The waves were rushing up the beach. I said, "Man they are big." David said, "Yeah they are. Don't forget to air up your

BC and don't get knocked down or you'll never get back up. Tell me when you're going. Let's try to stay close together so we can help each other if we need it." I said, "Okay" and started watching the waves.

We kept looking out at the waves and watching them. A big set came in. We watched them as they came rushing up toward us. A smaller wave started breaking. I said, "Now! Let's go." We both took off hurrying through the shallow water. We were walking fast and hurrying. Another wave broke, the water rushed up to us, the water was moving fast and hard. It hit my leg and twisted me around. I fell down and was getting knocked around. I knew I had to hurry up and get back on my feet. David grabbed my arm and helped me up. We kept hurrying out.

We were in water waist deep. We quickly put on our fins and mask then put our regulators in our mouths. We were kicking out fast and hurrying. A wave broke on us. We were rolling in the water getting washed back in. I looked up and over at David. He was holding onto his mask and regulator with his hands.

We started kicking out again. Another wave hit us. We were rolling back in again. I quickly reached up and started holding onto my mask and regulator.

I looked up and saw David. He's in front of me a little and over to my left. He was swimming with his arms and kicking out fast. I started swimming with my arms. We kept going as fast as we could. A wave started lifting me up. I didn't look at it. I kept my head in the water and kept going as fast as I could. I started thinking I hope I make it, I hope I make it. I was getting tired. The wave went under me. I went down the backside of it. I thought to myself I made it! I made it! I kept going as fast as I could. I looked up. David was still ahead of me. We were past where the waves are breaking. We slowed down and kept going.

We were out far enough that the waves wouldn't break on us. We stopped and took our regulators out of our mouths. I said, "I need to rest." David said, "Me too." We stayed close to each other. Water was splashing over our heads, as the waves would go past us. We were going up the waves then dropping down the backside of them. I said, "I think it would be easier on the bottom." David said, "Me too. I'm ready if you are." I said, "I'm ready."

We put our regulators back in our mouths. We started letting the air out of our BC's. We got close to the bottom but couldn't get on our hands and knees because the water was surging back and forth too much. The sand was all stirred up and the visibility was really bad. I looked around and set my compass, hoping it was a good heading. We started going out but the surge kept pulling us back in several feet and then pushing us out several feet.

I could see David's dive light but I couldn't see him very good. He was on my left side. We started going out, surging back and forth. We were slowly getting deeper and deeper. The deeper we were getting, the less surge there was and the better the visibility was getting. I could see David good now. We were going out fast sweeping with our dive lights. We were at forty feet. I had two thousand pounds of air.

I thought forty-six feet is where Deb and I went without getting lost. I started paying close attention to how deep we were getting and our heading. We kept going at our fast pace. David cut over right in front of me. I was thinking, "What's he doing?" I slowed down, got behind him and started following him. I checked our heading carefully to make sure we were still on the right heading so we wouldn't get lost again. I thought this is probably where we got lost before.

I looked back up and couldn't believe it! David had a bright yellow rope twisted and tangled up all around him! He was trying to get it off but the more he was trying to get it off the more it was twisting and tangling up around him. I thought how in the world could he get twisted up with that rope, that bad, that fast.

I went over to him. He stopped moving. I started untangling him. The rope looked like it was about forty or fifty feet long. David was finally free. David started going along the rope. It was tied to a boat anchor.

I checked my air. I was down to fifteen hundred pounds. I looked back over at David. He was rolling up the rope. He rolled it all up and tied it into a bundle. He left about ten feet of rope from the bundle to the anchor. David pointed in. I gave him the okay signal. David went down to the anchor, picked it up and grabbed the bundle of rope. We started going in.

I went over close to him and kept an eye on my compass. I made sure we were on our heading to go back in. David was on the open ocean side. He didn't look like he was having any trouble carrying the anchor and rope, but I knew it couldn't be very easy. The surge was gradually getting worse. We were at twenty-five feet. David signaled to go up. I gave him the okay signal. We slowly started going up.

We were on the surface. We took our regulators out of our mouths. Water was splashing over our heads. David's head was barely out of the water. The splashing was way over his head! The waves were just as big as before. We were going up, then down the waves.

David was getting water in his mouth and spitting it out while saying, "I'm going to take it in." I said, "Okay let me know if you need any help." David said, "Okay. I didn't want to get too close and the waves break on us so I came up early. Try to stay out of my way if you can." I said, "Okay." David said, "Watch the waves and tell me when to go." I said, "Okay" and started watching them. David put his regulator back in his mouth.

Some big waves went past us. It looked like the next waves were smaller. I said, "Now" and put my regulator back in my mouth. We both started kicking in, fast. I was staying on David's left side about fifteen feet from him. A wave broke on us but it wasn't too big. It pushed us in some. We kept kicking in. Another wave broke on us and pushed us in some more. David looked like he was doing okay. Another wave hit us but this one was big. It slammed me onto the bottom. I was rolling in the water. It pushed me way up on the beach. I got on my hands and knees. The water was rushing back past me. I stayed still and as steady as I could. I looked around for David but couldn't see him. The water was getting shallower and slowing down.

I quickly got up, hurried over to the steps and put my fins, mask and dive light on them. I turned around and could see David. I hurried over to him and said, "Give me the anchor." He gave it to me. He was carrying the rope, his fins, and dive light. We hurried over to the steps. I said, "Where's my other fin. A wave must have hit the steps and washed one away." David took his mask off and we started looking out in the water with our dive lights. David said, "There it is" and handed me the rope. The water was pulling it out. David hurried over to it, grabbed it out of the water then came back and got on the steps. I said, "I can't believe you made it with the anchor!" David said, "I let it hang down a few feet under me. If I got in trouble I was going to let it go and come in without it." I said, "That was a good idea but I still can't believe you made it in with it, in these big waves."

We started walking up the steps. David was carrying the anchor and rope. I carried our fins, masks and dive lights. We made it up the steps then walked over to the car. We took our dive gear off. I said, "You don't want to do another dive do you?" David said, "I think one was enough." I said, "Me too."

We took our wetsuits off. We loaded our dive gear, the anchor and the rope in the car. We were on our way to David's house. David said, "Do you think you can use that anchor on your boat?" I said, "I think it would be a perfect one for the boat." David said, "Good it's yours then." I said, "Okay."

We were getting close to David's house. I said, "I'll air up the tanks." David said, "Okay, are we going diving next weekend?" I said, "Yeah." David said, "I'm going to be busy Saturday so let's go Sunday." I said, "Okay." We drove up to David's house. He unloaded his dive gear. I went home, unloaded the tanks and my dive gear. I rinsed everything off and put it up.

Monday …

I loaded the two empty tanks in the car, drove to the dive shop, carried the tanks in and put them at the filling area. I walked to the front of the dive shop. Ron was behind the counter talking to a customer that was getting ready to buy something. I walked over and started looking at the books. I found one that was about beach dives. It looked like a good book so I started looking through it. It told short stories about the beaches and how to get to them. It had Shaw's Cove, Corona Del Mar and several other beaches. I was trying to remember the name of the beach that the dive shop does their deep dives at. Oh yeah! Redondo. I started looking for Redondo and found it. It showed you where to park and had a little map of the depths. It said Redondo is a submarine canyon and that there were only five places in Southern California that are close enough to do beach dives into the canyons. I thought I'm getting this book! I walked up to the counter.

Ron and the customer were talking about diving. Ron looked over at me and said, "Would you like to buy that book?" I said, "Yeah it looks like a good one and it has Redondo in it. Isn't that where you guys do the deep dives at?" Ron said, "Yes it is. That book has quite a few good diving locations in it." The customer said, "Are you going to Redondo? You usually won't see very much, but if you do see something, it's usually something you won't forget about. You'll probably even tell your grandkids about it. I saw a blue shark there once. It was nine feet long. Most divers don't believe me when I tell them though." I said, "It sounds like a neat place to dive." The customer said, "I really like diving there but most divers don't like it because it's deep and you don't see stuff very often." Ron said, "Be really careful there. It's really deep and you can get into trouble really easy." I said, "It sounds like fun I'm going to check it out." The customer said, "I'll tell you the way that I do it. I go straight out from the steps and kick out until I'm even with the end of the pier. That is where I go down at. It's close to the drop off into the canyon. Don't go out past the end of the pier or you'll go into the canyon." I said, "Okay I'll go down at the end of the pier."

I paid for the book then Ron started walking to the filling area. The customer and I followed Ron. Ron filled the tanks. I carried one tank and the book out to the car then walked back in and got the other tank. I said, "Thanks, Ron" then looked over at the customer and said, "Thanks for the information." I drove home and unloaded the tanks.

I called David and said, "I just bought a book that has Redondo in it. The dive shop does their deep dives there. I talked to Ron and some guy that likes diving there. It goes into a canyon where you can get real deep." David said, "That sounds like a good place to dive at. Let's go there Sunday." I said, "Okay." David said, "Let's go in the daytime and get familiar with it before we do night dives there." I said, "Okay do you want to do two dives?" David said, "Yeah." I said, "It sounded funny because he said most people don't like diving there because it's deep but he also said you don't see very much but when you do, it's something you don't forget about. He even said he saw a nine foot blue shark there once." David said, "If you can get deep, it must be fun." I said, "That's what I was thinking."

Chapter 4

Redondo Canyon

Sunday morning …

I called David and asked him if he was ready. David said he was. I said, "I'll be over in a few minutes." David said, "Okay." I loaded my dive gear in the car, drove to David's house and picked him up. I had a map opened up and sitting on the back seat next to the book. I picked up the map, started pointing at it and said, "It looks like it's here." David said, "That shouldn't be too hard to find." We were on our way to Redondo.

David started looking at the book and said, "This picture shows it going from the shore to over a hundred feet very quickly." I said, "I know. It looks like it's deep just a little distance out."

We kept driving along. David kept looking at the map and telling me where to turn. We were getting close. David said, "The book says there's a parking lot on the right." We started looking for it. David said, "There. That parking lot must be it."

We drove in. The parking lot was crowded with divers. Everywhere you looked they were behind their cars with their dive gear. They were putting their dive gear together or putting on their wetsuits. It seemed like everyone was so busy. David and I finally found a parking spot and parked.

We got out and looked around then started walking around asking people about diving there. Most of the people we talked to were students and didn't know anything about it. One student said, "It's sandy." We could hear a guy telling divers that they would be going in soon. David and I walked over to him. He looked like an instructor. David said, "Are we at the right place? We're looking for a place where it's suppose to be deep." The instructor said, "Yeah, You're at the right place. Just go out past the students where you look down toward the pier. When you're past the end of the pier, you're in deep water. We don't let the students go out that far." David said, "Oh good. I was surprised to see students here." The instructor said, "It's a good place for training just as long as you stay above the drop off." David said, "Thanks." The instructor said, "Be careful! You can get in trouble out there." David said, "Okay."

David and I walked to the edge of the parking lot where there are some steps going down to the beach. We started looking around at the beach and the ocean. At the bottom of the steps was a wide sidewalk along the beach where people were jogging, walking, riding bikes and skating. It looked like it was going to be an easy place for us to go in at. All we would have to do is walk down the steps, across the sidewalk then across the beach to the water. We could see the pier to the right about a block away. David looked down at a brick building that was next to the bottom of the steps and said, "I think that's a restroom." I said, "Good - and look! It has showers too." The showers are mounted on the outside wall.

We walked back to the car, unloaded our dive gear and put it together. We put our wetsuits on. I helped David with his hood. We opened up our air and checked our regulators then put our dive gear on. David asked, "Are you ready?" I said, "I'm ready."

We grabbed our fins and mask, walked to the steps and went down them. We walked across the sidewalk and started looking around for a good place to go in at. We didn't want to get in the way of the classes. There were three groups of classes out in the water not far from the shore, with about eight to ten divers in each group. David said, "Let's go in over there" and started pointing to the left of the students. I said, "Okay." The surf was small and it was going to be easy to get in.

We walked over, closer to the water, to an area that has a few rocks. There weren't any rocks around anywhere except for these, for some reason. David asked, "Are you ready?" I said, "Yeah." We aired up our BC's and got in. I said, "Wow! There's a drop off all ready." It was a small drop off, about a foot or so deep, that almost made me fall as soon as I stepped into the water.

We put our fins on and started kicking out. I said, "The guy at the dive shop said to go out to where we look down at the end of the pier and that's where the drop off into the canyon is." David said, "Let's go down before we get there then and check it out." I said, "Okay."

We kept kicking out. We looked over at the pier, we were a little over half way. I said, "What do you think about here?" David said, "This looks good to me and I think we're out of the way of the students." I said, "What's our dive plan?" David said, "Let's go straight out as far as we can, then start back in when we're down to fifteen hundred pounds. Since you've got the compass I'll stay next to you." I said, "Okay, straight out and straight in." I set my compass.

We put our mask on, our regulators in our mouths and started letting the air out of our BC's. We started slowly going down staying close together. The visibility was about twenty feet. We kept going down and down. I could finally see the bottom.

We got down to the bottom, got on our knees and gave each other the okay signal. We were twenty-eight feet deep. It was a sandy bottom with no rocks, no reef, nothing but sand. I checked my compass then pointed out, showing David which way to go. David gave me the okay signal. We started going slowly, staying close to the bottom. We were popping our ears often. I was thinking at Shaw's Cove you can go a long way before popping your ears but here you have to pop them often. We looked up ahead. It was starting to get darker. We slowed down even more. We can see it! It's the drop off. It was lit up behind us, but over the drop off it was a lot darker.

We slowly went up to the edge, stopped and looked down over it. It was steep and it looked just like dirt. I thought man, this looks a little scary! It was a steep drop off going down about twenty or thirty feet then at the bottom it flattened out. David and I gave each other the okay signal. We started going down the drop off. It was dirt with some kind of weed-like stuff growing on it. We slowly kept going down, popping our ears every few feet.

We were at the bottom of the drop off. We looked out toward the deep water. It looked flat with no sand now, just dirt. Nothing was growing anywhere and there were no rocks or anything, just flat dirt. It looked sort of like a flat desert. I looked straight up and could only see water with our bubbles going up and fading out of sight.

I checked my compass and pointed out to David. We started slowly going out. I couldn't believe it, it was so open and nothing but dirt. I checked my air. I was down to twenty two hundred pounds. I checked our depth - we were already at eighty feet! I thought oh my gosh! It looks flat. But, it must be a slope since we're already this deep. We kept going out. David started pointing. There was a bat ray in front of us sitting on the bottom. We went toward it and got close to it. It swam away, stirring up a lot of the dirt. We were at a hundred and five feet. I still had nineteen hundred pounds of air. We were still going out. I could hear boat motors but I couldn't tell which direction they were going or where they were. I checked my air. I was down to fifteen hundred pounds. We were at a hundred and eighteen feet. I signaled to David for us to turn around. He gave me the okay signal.

We turned around and started back in. We were looking around. I was thinking how neat it was, being so deep so close to shore. I looked straight up. It seemed like it was an endless amount of water over us.

We were gradually getting shallower. We could see the drop off coming up ahead of us. From this direction, it looked like it was a wall that was almost straight up and down. We went up to the drop off and started up it. I started floating up and getting out of control. I started swimming down and dumping air out of my BC really quick.

Finally, I was neutral. I got on my knees on the side of the drop off. I started going up again. I was dumping air out of my BC and slowly going up the drop off. We made it to the top, turned around and looked back down. It looked neat but it sure was dark and gloomy. We started going along the sandy bottom while going in. David pointed for us to go up. I gave him the okay signal. We got close together and started up, staying close together.

We were on the surface. We aired up our BC's, took our regulators out of our mouths and our mask off. David said, "I didn't want us to get in the way of the dive classes. That's why I wanted us to come up early." I said, "I forgot about the classes. Man, that was neat! You can get as deep as you want here, easy." David said, "I know I like this place." I said, "Me too."

We kicked around past the students and started kicking in toward where we came in at. We were close to shore. We took our fins off and got out. David said, "Let's rinse off in the showers." I said, "Okay." We walked to the showers. We just stood there under the showers with the water running over our heads. The cold water felt so good. We were hot and it was cooling us off. After a few minutes David asked, "Are you ready?" I said, "Yeah." We walked up the steps then over to the car. We took our dive gear and wetsuits off then changed tanks.

David said, "I sure could use a cup of coffee now. I think I saw a place to get some as we were driving in. I think I'll walk over there and see." He started pointing across the street. I said, "Get me a cup too." David said, "Okay" and started walking.

David walked back with two cups of coffee and said, "It's not too far but I sure did feel stupid in there wearing a wet bathing suit." I started laughing and said, "I bet you looked a little stupid too!" We drank our coffee then David said, "How's our surface interval doing? Can we do our next dive yet?" I checked the computer and said, "It shows the maximum dive time at a hundred feet. So it looks to me like we're ready." David said, "Let's go then."

We put our wetsuits and dive gear back on, walked across the parking lot, down the steps then across the beach close to where we went in on our first dive.

David said, "Let's just do the same thing we did on our first dive." I said, "Okay." We got in, put our fins on and kicked out past the students. David said, "Let's go out a little further this time before going down." I said, "Okay."

We looked down at the pier. We were almost even with the end of it. David said, "I think this is about right." I said, "Okay. Let's go." I set my compass. We put our masks on, our regulators in our mouths and started letting the air out of our BC's. We were going down staying together, popping our ears along the way. We were going down and down. I could see the bottom gradually getting closer.

We were on the bottom. The drop off was right next to us only about ten feet further out. We gave each other the okay signal, went over to the edge of the drop and stopped. We looked down the dark drop off. I pointed down the drop off. David gave me the okay signal. We started slowly going down the drop off. We got to the bottom of it. I checked my compass and pointed out. David gave me the okay signal.

We were going out and looking around. It is so flat looking. I kept checking my depth as we were getting deeper and deeper. We were going straight out but at a faster pace this time. We were just looking around at the dirt bottom while we were going along. David started pointing at something. It's some kind of jar and it has something in it. We kicked over to it. There is something dark inside. David picked it up and started looking in it, then he started showing it to me. It was an octopus! I thought how weird. I guess that's the only place it can hide out here. David put it back down.

I checked our depth. We were at a hundred and five feet. We started going out again. I looked to my left. It was another bat ray swimming off, stirring up the dirt like the other one did.

I checked my air. I was down to fifteen hundred pounds. We were at a hundred and twenty one feet. I signaled to David for us to turn around. He gave me the okay signal. We turned around and started back in. We kept going, looking around. We can see the bottom of the drop off coming up. I had nine hundred pounds of air. We went up the drop off about halfway then I pointed for us to turn right and go along the side of the drop off wall. David gave me the okay signal. We turned and started looking at the drop off. There is a few things growing on it, but not much, it was mostly just dirt.

I checked my air. I was down to five hundred pounds. I signaled to David to start going up. We went to the top of the drop off. I was down to four hundred pounds of air. I signaled to David for us to go up. He gave me the okay signal. We started going up.

We were on the surface. We aired up our BC's, took our regulators out of our mouths and our mask off. We looked down toward the pier. We were right at the end of it. David said, "I really like this place. This is really fun." I said, "I know I like it too. I like diving deep and it's so easy here." David said, "It is." We kicked around past the students and started kicking in toward where we came in at.

We were close to shore. We took our fins off and got out. We walked up to the showers and started rinsing off again. It felt so good with the cold water running over our heads. We just stood there under the water. People would walk up rinse off and leave but we kept standing there letting it run over us. David said, "I'm ready when you are." I said, "I'm ready."

We walked up the steps and to the car. We took our dive gear and wetsuits off. I said, "I can't believe we did a hundred and eighteen feet and a hundred and twenty one feet dive just a little way off the beach." David said, "I know. It's deep here. How about doing a night dive here Friday night?" I said, "Okay. Do you want to do two?" David said, "Okay."

We loaded the dive gear in the car and started home. David said, "Let's stop and get something to eat. I'm hungry." I said, "Okay, how about a hamburger?" David said, "Okay." We drove through the fast food drive though. I ordered for us then said, "Oh no! I don't have any money. I locked it up in the trunk." David said, "I'll get it. You always get the air." I said, "Okay."

We got our food then started home. David said, "I think I'll get a computer and compass like you have. Let me know the next time you're going to the dive shop and I'll go with you." I said, "Let's go tomorrow." David said, "Okay."

Monday …

David called and said he was ready to go to the dive shop. I told him I was too. He said he would come and pick me up. David drove up. We loaded the tanks in his truck then drove to the dive shop. We carried the tanks in and put them at the filling area. Eddie started filling them. David and I walked up to the front. Ron was behind the counter. Ron said, "Hello." David said, "Hello. I want to order a computer and a compass in a console like Lee has." Ron said, "Sure." David said, "Will the pressure gauge that I already have fit in the console?" Ron pointed at a pressure gauge in a glass cabinet under the counter and said, "Is it this size?" David said, "Yes." Ron said, "It'll fit." David said, "Good." Ron started filling out the paperwork and said, "It will take about a week to get. We'll call you when it comes in." David said, "Okay."

A guy walked in the front door carrying two tanks and took them back to Eddie. He walked back up to the front and got next to the counter by us. David said to Ron, "We went to Redondo yesterday. I really like it there." Ron said, "It's deep there." David said, "Yeah, that's what I like about it." The guy said, "I don't like it there. I like it where the lobsters are but Ben likes it there. He dives there all the time. He even claims he saw a shark there once. That's what he claims anyway." David said, "What kind of shark?" The guy said, "He claims it was a nine foot blue shark." I said to Ron, "That's the same guy that was here when I bought the book, isn't it?" Ron said, "Yeah, that's him." I said, "That would be scary to see a big shark like that." Ron said, "You need to be really careful diving there."

The guy started asking Ron some questions about his equipment. David and I walked to the back. Eddie was filling the other guys tanks and said, "Yours are all full." I said, "Thanks, Eddie." We loaded the tanks in the truck. David took me home. I said, "You want to leave your tanks here?" David said, "Yeah let's keep them all together." We unloaded the tanks and put them up.

Tuesday …

Deb called and said, "Let's go diving." I said, "I can't today but I can tomorrow. David and I went to Redondo. It's neat. You can get deep really fast, not far from shore." Deb said, "What did you see?" I said, "Nothing much, mostly just dirt and sand but we did see two bat rays and an octopus." Deb said, "I think I would rather do a night dive at Shaw's Cove. We know we'll see a lot there." I said, "Okay, let's go tomorrow."

Wednesday evening …

I called Deb and said, "It's night dive time." Deb said, "I'm ready. Pick me up." I loaded the dive gear, drove to Deb's house and picked her up. We were on our way to Shaw's Cove. I said, "It was really fun at Redondo. We did two dives and they were both around a hundred and twenty feet." Deb said, "That is deep. I'm off today and tomorrow. Let's go there tomorrow." I said, "Okay but it will have to be tomorrow morning. Do you want to do two dives?" Deb said, "Okay." I said, "We'll have to get air first." Deb said, "Okay come by and pick me when you're ready." I said, "Okay."

It was almost dark. We drove by where we could see the ocean. Deb started trying to look at the waves. She couldn't see them very well. Deb said, "I think the waves are small." I said, "Good. The last dive I did here with David they were really big."

We drove up at Shaw's Cove, parked and got out. We could hear the waves. Deb said, "Good they sound small." We unloaded our dive gear and put it together. We cracked open our chemsticks, tied them to our tanks, opened up our air and checked our regulators. We started putting our wetsuits on. I started looking around at the nice big expensive houses that are around there. I said, "You know, it's funny how calm and peaceful this neighborhood is then just a few feet out in the water, it's like going to a zoo where all the animals are loose!" Deb said, "Yeah! I wish I owned one of these houses." I said, "Me too." Deb said, "Let's go down as soon as we can and just look at everything." I said, "Okay." We put our dive gear on.

We walked to the steps and down to the beach. It was really dark, no moon and there were hardly any lights on anywhere. It was really quiet and gloomy. Deb said, "Man is it quiet." I said, "It sure is." We aired up our BC's, turned on our dive lights, got in the water and put our fins on. Deb said, "Let's go down here." The water was only about five feet deep. We were next to the reef and could still touch. I said, "Okay."

We put our mask on, our regulators in our mouths and let the air out of our BC's. We were just barely underwater. We gave each other the okay signal. Deb started going out next to the reef. She was shining her dive light on it, going slowly, while looking into every crack in the reef she came up to. I was next to her and looking at everything too. We could see fish hiding way up in some of the cracks, just sleeping. We kept going really slow, taking our time and looking around.

I looked over toward the open ocean and on the sand was a flat fish. I went up next to Deb and pointed over at it. We went over close to it. It was about two and a half feet long with a flat round head with thorn-like things on it's back. It was shaped like a banjo. We looked at it and left it alone. We went back over to the reef and started looking at it again. We kept looking in the cracks. Deb started waving at me. I went up next to her. She was pointing in front of us about five feet. It looked like a dead lobster. Deb went up to it and picked it up. She turned it upside down. It was empty. It was like the skin of a lobster. She put it back down. We went out a little further. I checked my air. I was down to fifteen hundred pounds. We were at thirty-two feet. I signaled to Deb for us to turn around and start back in. She gave me the okay signal.

We turned around and started back in. We were going slow, looking at the reef. We were taking our time, getting shallower and shallower. I checked our depth. We were at twelve feet. We kept going in. I could see the surface of the water real good now. We were four feet deep. We stuck our heads out of the water and aired up our BC's. Deb said, "That is so neat at night but it seems darker tonight for some reason." I said, "I know it seems a little bit strange tonight too." Deb said, "I think a lobster must have shedded because that didn't look like a lobster body." I said, "It was pretty weird looking. That flat fish was weird too with that big round head." Deb said, "Yeah, it was."

I asked, "Are you ready to get out?" Deb said, "Yeah. I'm ready." We took our fins off and got out. Deb handed me her weights, mask and fins. We slowly walked up the steps and back up to the car. We took our dive gear and wetsuits off. We packed everything in the car. We were on our way to Deb's house.

We drove up to Deb's house. She unloaded her dive gear and said, "I'll see you in the morning." I said, "Okay" and drove home. I unloaded my dive gear, rinsed it off and put it up.

Thursday morning …

I called Deb and asked her if she was ready. She said she was. I said, "I'm on my way." I loaded my dive gear in the car then drove to Deb's house. Deb loaded her dive gear.

We were on our way to the dive shop. As we drove up I said, "Hey! There's Kate's car." We parked, carried the tanks in and put them at the filling area. We walked up to the front. Eddie said, "I'll fill your tanks" and started walking to the filling area. I said, "Thanks Eddie."

Kate was talking to Ron. Deb and I walked over to them and started talking with them. I said to Kate, "David and I went to Redondo and we really liked it. Now Deb and I are going." Kate said, "Can I go with you guys? I've got all my dive gear with me in my car." Deb said, "Sure." Kate said, "I'll follow you guys down there." Deb said, "Okay."

Eddie walked back up to the front and said, "Your tanks are full." I said, "Thanks Eddie. We'll see guys later." I said to Kate, "Are you ready?" Kate said, "I'll be right behind you." Deb and I walked back to the filling area. We carried the tanks to the car and loaded them. Kate got in her car. We were on our way to Redondo. Kate was following us.

We drove into the parking lot and parked. There was a lot of parking and no students. Kate parked next to us. We unloaded our dive gear and put it together. We opened up our air and checked our regulators. Kate asked, "Are you guys ready to put your wetsuits on?" Deb and I said yes. We all started putting them on. I said, "David and I are going to do two night dives here tomorrow night. Do you guys want to go?" Deb said, "I can't. I've got to work." Kate said, "Sure I like night diving. Call me when you're ready and I'll meet you down here." I said, "Okay."

We finished putting our wetsuits on then put our dive gear on. We walked over to the steps then down to the beach and close to the water. Kate said, "Air up your BC's." Deb and I looked at each other while airing them up. It seemed like Kate thought she was in charge of us like we were still students. I thought since Deb and I are pretty new and she was a trainee dive instructor, she's probably feeling like she's responsible for us but she seemed a little stressed out about it. Deb said to Kate, "Why don't you lead and we will follow you." Kate said, "Okay." I looked straight out from the beach and set my compass. We got in the water, put our fins on and started kicking out.

We were about half way out to the end of the pier. I said, "When we're even with the end of the pier, that's where the drop off is." Deb said, "Let's go down here." Kate looked at me. I said, "This is fine with me if it is with you." Kate said, "This is fine with me." Deb said, "Let's go." We put our mask on then Deb grabbed her power inflater and let a little bit of air out of her BC. She said, "Oh no, I almost forgot to put my regulator in my mouth." I started laughing. Kate looked at Deb and said loudly, "Don't forget to put your regulator in your mouth." Deb and I looked at each other again. We all put our regulators in our mouths, got close together and slowly started letting the air out of our BC's. We were going down.

We were on the bottom and got on our knees. We all gave each other the okay signal. Kate started going. Deb got on her left side and I got on her right side. We were going along slowly, staying close to the bottom. I started floating up away from the bottom so I let some air out of my BC. That way, I would stay close to bottom. I was thinking this is weird. Usually, I have to add air when we're going out, something is strange.

I checked our depth. We kept going. A little further I checked our depth again. We were getting shallower. We were going the wrong way! We're going in. I waved at Kate to stop. We all stopped. I signaled to Kate that we were going in the wrong direction, we needed to turn around to go out. She gave me the okay signal. We all turned around and started going out. I waved at Kate, pointed to my compass and then to me, like I want to navigate. Kate gave me the okay signal. I moved over between Deb and Kate. I started navigating.

We kept going, looking around at the sandy bottom as it was gradually getting deeper and deeper. We could see the dark area from the drop off coming up. We slowed down, went up to the edge of the drop off and stopped. We looked down it, then we all gave each other the okay signal. I pointed down the drop off and started going down it. We went down the drop off then started going out from the bottom of it. Deb and Kate were staying next to me. We kept going out looking around at the dirt bottom getting deeper and deeper.

Kate waved at me and showed me her computer. It had a bunch of different digital numbers on it. I didn't know what I was looking at. I could see the numbers but I wasn't sure which numbers were what. I looked at her and gave her the okay signal to see if she was okay. She gave me the okay signal back. I thought everything must be okay. I pointed out deeper. Kate gave me the okay signal.

I checked our depth. We were at ninety-five feet. Everything was going well. We kept going deeper. I saw something out of the corner of my eye, then I felt my mask get knocked off my head. It felt like something pushed it off. I held my breathe, quickly dumped all the air out of my BC, got on my knees and told myself, be calm, don't choke on the water, don't breathe in through my nose, don't panic. Everything was blurry. I slowly breathed in through my mouth being careful not to breathe in through my nose, then slowly breathed out of my mouth, I slowly breathed in and out again. I was concentrating on each breath. Kate put my mask in my hand. I was keeping my eyes wide open and didn't blink any. I slowly put my mask up against my face still concentrating on breathing. I slowly pushed the mask strap over my head. My mask was on my head but it was full of water. I pushed in on the front of it with my fingers and slowly breathed out of my nose. The water level slowly dropped down a little in my mask. I slowly breathed in again then slowly breathed out of my nose again. The water level went down some more. It was less then halfway full of water now. I slowly breathed in again then slowly breathed out of my nose again. All the water drained out. I was so happy and thought I did it, I did it! My mask was completely off and I put it back on at a hundred feet without any problem!

I could see Kate moving around. She started waving at me. She took her regulator out of her mouth, dropped it down to her side and was giving me the out of air signal. I thought oh crap, she's out of air. I quickly grabbed my back-up regulator and started breathing with it. I quickly handed her my regulator. She started breathing with it. She gave me the okay signal. I gave it back. I thought that's probably why my mask got knocked off. She must have run out of air, was trying to tell me and accidentally knocked it off.

We kept using my regulators. I looked over at Deb everything seemed to be okay. I checked my air. I was already down to eight hundred pounds. I thought we have to go straight up. We don't have enough air to go in on the bottom. Deb and I haven't gone straight up from a hundred feet before, I doubt if Kate has either. There's no choice we have to go straight up. I looked back over at Deb and pointed up. She gave me the okay signal. I pointed up to Kate. She gave me the okay signal.

Kate and I grabbed onto each other's BC straps. We got face to face. I felt awkward because my back-up regulator is in my mouth but since it's also my power inflator I can't see the buttons to air up or dump air out of my BC. I started feeling for the buttons. I felt the small button to add air. I pushed it and added some air to my BC.

We started up. I was kicking and kicking while watching our depth. We weren't going up any. I felt my fins hitting the bottom. I started to panic a little and think why aren't we going up? I've never had trouble going up before! What is happening? I added a lot of air to my BC and kept kicking. We still weren't going up! I could feel my heart starting to beat super fast. I added a lot more air to my BC until my dump valve started popping off. I knew this was it! My BC was as full as it could be. We had to get off the bottom this time! I started kicking up as hard and as fast as I could. Finally, we slowly started going up. I thought what a relief! We kept slowly going up.

Kate and I were holding onto each other's BC straps tight. Deb was about five feet away on my left side. We were going up but I could tell the more we were going up, the faster we were going. I quickly grabbed my computer and looked at it. It was flashing *Slow, Slow, Slow*. We were going up too fast!

I quickly started feeling around on my backup regulator for the big button so I could let some air out of my BC. I could feel my dump valve on my BC popping off. The air in my BC must have expanded from going up. I found my big button and completely pushed it in and held it. It was wide open, dumping air out of my BC.

We were still going up way too fast. I thought the air in Kate's BC must have expanded too and she must not be dumping any air out of it. We were going up, fast. I checked our depth we were at thirty feet. The computer is still flashing *Slow, Slow, Slow*. I looked up. It seemed like we were flying up through the water.

We shot up to the surface. I aired up my BC. Kate and I took our regulators out of our mouths. We both just floated on the surface. Kate started moaning a little. After several seconds, Deb came up and said, "You guy's went up really fast." I said, "I couldn't control us. First I couldn't get us off the bottom, then I couldn't slow us down." Kate started burping really loud and long. She didn't look very good. I said, "Are you all right?" Kate said, "I don't think so. Let me rest a little bit." I said, "Okay."

We kept floating around and not moving much. After a few minutes Kate said, "Let's kick in slow and try to get out." Deb and I said, "Okay." We slowly started kicking in.

We kicked in close to the shore, took our fins off, got out and started walking across the beach. I was on Kate's right side and Deb was on her left side. We slowly walked across the beach, up the steps and over to the cars.

We took our dive gear and wetsuits off then sat down on the ground behind the cars. Several minutes later I said to Kate, "How are you feeling?" Kate said, "Believe it or not I'm feeling a little better. I didn't think I was going to make it for awhile though." I said, "Do you think you'll be able to do another dive?" Kate said, "I might be able too. Let me rest and I'll let you know." I said, "Okay. I haven't ever had to completely put my mask on underwater much less at a hundred feet." Deb said, "We always talked about practicing putting them on underwater but we never did it." I said, "I know I wish we would have. I was a little worried." Kate said, "I ran out of air and accidentally knocked your mask off. Then, I had to hold my breath and wait for you to put your mask on before I could let you know I was out of air." Deb said, "And you took forever to put it on." Kate said, "I know! You did!" I said, "You're kidding? You held your breath that whole time?" Kate said, "Yeah." I said, "When you showed me your computer were you telling me you were low on air?" Kate said, "Yes, I only had five hundred pounds." I said, "I could see a lot of numbers but I couldn't tell what I was looking at." Kate said, "I should have just gave the signal to come back in."

We rested a little longer, then Deb and I got up. We started changing tanks. Kate started changing hers. I checked my computer. It showed the maximum time at a hundred feet. I said, "My computer shows we're okay to do our next dive." Kate said, "I'm feeling a lot better now." I asked, "Do you want to do another dive?" Kate said, "Yeah but let's not go too deep. Let's just stay on the sand and not go down the drop off." Deb and I said okay. I said, "Let us know when you're ready." Kate said, "I'm ready how about you guys?" I said, "I'm ready." Deb said, "Me too."

We put our wetsuits and dive gear on. We walked across the parking lot, down the steps and across the beach. I said, "Deb, put your regulator in your mouth before you go down this time." We all laughed. I looked straight out and checked my compass. Kate said, "Air up your BC's." We aired them up, got in and put our fins on. We kicked out a little way. Deb said, "Why don't we just go down and go out on the bottom since we're going to stay shallow." Kate and I said okay. We put our mask on, our regulators in our mouths and slowly started letting the air out of our BC's.

We were on the bottom. We were twelve feet deep. We gave each other the okay signal. I moved over between Deb and Kate. I pointed out. I kept checking my compass to make sure we were going out. We were going slow and straight out. We were looking at the sand and around to see if there was anything to catch our eye.

All of a sudden, something was happening, something was going on! We started looking at each other. We all stopped and got on our knees on the bottom. It's fish. It started getting dark. It's a giant school of fish. Fish were everywhere! They were just like soldiers marching. We were looking out toward the deep water. They were coming from our left and going to the right. They were all about twelve to fourteen inches long and about a foot and a half away from each other, from front to back, up and down and side to side. Not one was out of place except where they were going around us and our air bubbles. Then they were getting right back in their places. They were as far as we could see in every direction from the bottom going up to the surface and as far in toward the shore and as far out as we could see.

We stayed still and looked at each other. We couldn't believe what we were seeing. I thought this is one of the most amazing things I've ever seen. The fish just kept going around us. We kept watching them.

We could see the end of them coming. It started to get more lit up. As the last ones were going past I quickly looked from the shallow water to the deep water. The back of them were perfectly lined up, perfectly straight - not any of them out of place.

We stayed still and watched them go past. We kept watching until they faded out of sight. I thought that couldn't have been real. We all looked at each other. Our eyes were as big as saucers and wide open! We kept looking in that direction but all we could see was water.

I pointed out. Deb and Kate gave me the okay signal. We slowly started going. We came up to the drop off and turned left. We went along the top of the drop off, looking down it, then back across the sand. I checked my air. I was down to nine hundred pounds. I pointed in. Deb and Kate gave me the okay signal. We turned and started going in. We were slowly going across the sandy bottom.

We were at fourteen feet. I pointed up. Deb and Kate gave me the okay signal. We went up. We took our regulators out of our mouths and our mask off. I said, "That was the biggest school of fish I've ever seen. I've never even heard of a school of fish being that big!" Deb said, "That was so amazing. There were so many fish!" Kate said, "I know. That was unbelievable!" I said, "I bet it was at least as big as a football field." Deb said, "I know it was big." Kate said, "It was."

We kept talking about the school of fish and the dive for awhile then I said, "Are you guys ready to get out?" Deb and Kate both said yes. We kicked in close, took our fins off and got out. Deb handed me her weights, mask and fins. We walked over to the showers, rinsed off then we walked up to the cars. We took off our dive gear and wetsuits.

We loaded everything into our cars. Kate said, "Thanks for letting me go with you guys." Deb and I said, "You're welcome." Kate said to me, "Call me tomorrow and I'll meet you down here." I said, "Okay."

We were on our way to Deb's house. Deb said, "I'm off Tuesday let's come back then." I said, "Okay." We drove up to Deb's house. Deb unloaded her dive gear. I drove home, unloaded my dive gear and rinsed it off.

Friday morning …

I loaded the tanks in the car and drove to the dive shop. I carried the tanks in and put them at the filling area then walked up to the front. Ron, Kate and a guy I've never seen before were all behind the counter talking. Ron said, "I heard you saw a big school of fish." I said, "We did. It was a real big school of fish." Kate said, "It was really neat." I said, "I didn't know a school of fish could be that big." Kate looked over at Ron and said, "You wouldn't believe how much Lee's been diving." Ron said, "I've got a good idea. We've aired up a bunch of his tanks." I said, "I've been diving every chance I get."

I looked up at one of the dry erase boards behind the counter. It had "Three Day Channel Islands Dive Trip" at the top and some names written under it. Ron said, "You should go to the Channel Islands. There are still some openings." Kate said, "I'm going and Danny is too." She was pointing at the guy next to her. Ron said, "It's a lot of fun." I asked, "What are the Channel Islands?" Ron said, "They're the islands out from Santa Barbara. It's a really fun trip, especially on this boat. You'll do a lot of different dives up there and the visibility is really good. Danny is our dive shop representative." I said, "It sounds like fun to me. Sign me up. I'm working, but I need a vacation." Danny said, "Okay." Ron walked to the back of the dive shop and started filling my tanks.

Danny got out a notebook, showed me a diagram of the boat and said, "Which bunk do you want? We have the bunks from the center to the left side" then he pointed to the bunks that were still available. I said, "Which ones are the best?" Kate said, "I picked this one" and started pointing to one against the side of the boat. Then she pointed to some in the center and said, "I don't like these." I pointed to the one over Kate's bunk and asked, "Is this one available?" Danny said, "Yeah, that's a good one too. It's a wide one. You'll have plenty of room there." I said, "I'll take that one."

Danny said, "You'll have a lot of fun. It's about a hundred miles, so if you can carpool with someone or you can go with me because I'm taking my van. I'm going the night before though so that I can sleep all night." I said to Kate, "Do you know how to get there?" Kate said, "Yes." I asked, "Do you want to carpool? I'll drive." Kate said, "Sure." Danny said, "Be real quiet when you get there because people will be sleeping on the boat. I'll be one of them." Kate and I said okay.

I started looking at the dry erase board that was to the right of the Channel Island one. It had "Catalina Underwater Park" and had a long list of names under it. Ron walked up and said to me, "Your tanks are full." I said, "Okay, thanks Ron." I said, "What's the Catalina Underwater Park?" Danny said, "It's the dive park at Catalina. It's roped off like a swimming area but you're not allowed to swim there - only dive. It's next to the casino over there. It's deep. You'll like it too." I said, "Why is it so cheap?" Ron said, "It's a beach dive. If you sign up, we'll pay for the boat trip along with your dive gear to be hauled from the boat to the beach and back." I said, "That's so inexpensive! I have to go and check it out. Sign me up for that one too."

Danny said to me, "You've been doing a lot of diving?" I said, "Every chance I get I go." Danny said, "I know a girl that needs a lot of dives before she goes to Florida. She just got certified and has to have several dives in. She only has a couple of weeks before she leaves. She's going to be living in an underwater laboratory. Her name is Kirsten." I said, "Tell her if she needs someone to dive with to let me know." Danny said, "I can do that. Can I give her your number?" I said, "Sure." Danny said, "Why don't I call her now." I said, "Okay. Go ahead." Danny called her then said to me, "She said she would like to go tomorrow if that's okay." I said, "Yeah. Ask her if she wants to meet here at the dive shop." Danny said, "Yeah. She said that's okay. Is around 10:00 all right?" I said, "Yeah. Tell her I'll see her here." Danny hung up the phone and said, "Thanks Lee." I said, "No problem. I'll see you guys later." I walked to the back of the dive shop, carried the tanks out to the car and drove home.

Later that evening …

I called David and said, "I hope it's okay with you that I invited Kate to go with us tonight." David said, "That's fine with me." I said, "Even though she's an instructor we need to sort of keep an eye on her." David said, "What do you mean?" I said, "Deb and I went to Redondo with her yesterday. Kate was navigating at first. She had us going in instead of out. That wasn't any big deal because I did it once too but then she ran out of air at a hundred feet. When she was trying to let me know she was out of air she accidentally knocked my mask off!" David said, "You had your mask knocked off at a hundred feet by a girl dive instructor that ran out of air and we're doing a deep night dive with her tonight!" I started laughing and said, "Yeah, but don't worry because I told her you can hold your breath a long time!" David said, "Sounds like I might have to tonight." I said, "Plus she uses her air up faster than I do. I think she might get nervous when she goes deep diving." David said, "This should be exciting." I said, "You wouldn't believe the school of fish we saw. It was huge! It was at least as big as a football field." David said, "Deb told me you guys saw a big school of fish." I said, "I signed up to go on a three day boat dive trip to the Channel Islands and a trip to Catalina to do a beach dive. There's a dive park next to that casino that you see in most pictures of Catalina. Do you want to go with me on them?" David said, "I better not go this time but if you like it and go again let me know and I'll try to go with you next time." I said, "Okay. I'll let you know if they're any good or not." David said, "Okay and we'll just keep an eye on Kate. I'm ready when you are." I said that I was ready and I would come over and pick him up.

I loaded my dive gear and called Kate. I told her that I was leaving to pick up David and then we'd be on our way." Kate said, "Okay. I'll meet you guys down there." I said, "We'll probably stop and get something to eat on the way down there." Kate said, "Okay. I will too. I'll see you soon." I said, "Okay."

I drove over to David's house and picked him up. We were on our way to Redondo. We drove through a fast food restaurant and got tacos and sodas. Then we drove to the beach and parked close to the steps. There weren't any divers around and the parking lot wasn't very crowded.

The sun was just going down and it was starting to get dark. We walked up close to the steps and looked out at the waves. David said, "Good, the waves are small and it's going to be nice and dark. Let's go eat." I said, "Okay." We walked back to the car. Kate drove up and parked next to us. She had Mexican food too. We all started eating.

We finished eating then unloaded our dive gear and put it together. We broke open our chemsticks and tied them to our tanks. I said to Kate, "What do you think about kicking out close to the end of the pier, go down, then David and I will get on each side of you. Then go straight out until someone gets down to fifteen hundred pounds then just point to your pressure gauge, we'll turn around and start back in." David and Kate said that was okay with them. We put on our wetsuits. I went over and helped David with his hood. We put our dive gear on, walked over to the steps, went down them then across the beach. David said, "Don't forget to air up your BC's." We all aired them up and turned on our dive lights. I checked my compass. We got in, put our fins on and started kicking out.

We looked down toward the pier. We were about three fourths of the way out to the end of it. I said, "How's this? This way we'll have plenty of time to get ready and get together before we go down the drop off." David and Kate said, "Okay." We put our mask on, our regulators in our mouths and started letting the air out of our BC's. We were all going down slow while staying close together.

We were on the bottom. We gave each other the okay signal. We were at twenty-eight feet. I got on Kate's left side and David got on her right side. I checked my compass then pointed out. David and Kate gave me the okay signal. We started going out slow taking our time. David and I were sweeping slowly with our dive lights from our sides to in front of Kate. Kate started sweeping with hers in front of David and I, back and forth. We could see in front of us and next to us really good this way. We could see the drop off coming up. We went up to the edge of it and stopped. We started looking down it. It was dark, very dark. I looked over at David and Kate and gave them the okay signal. They gave it back. We slowly started going down the drop off, sweeping with our dive lights. We got to the bottom of the drop off and stopped. We started shining our dive lights out toward the deep water. It looked very dark and scary. We didn't see anything moving but it didn't seem like we were alone. I checked my compass. David and Kate were looking at me. I pointed out. David and Kate gave me the okay signal.

We started slowly going along the bottom. The visibility was okay but we could only see where our dive lights were shining and only for about ten feet or so. We kept going, slowly. Some dirt was stirred up ahead of us. We slowly went toward it and went through it. I thought something must have been there and suddenly took off when it saw us, which stirred up the dirt. I was getting nervous and wondered, "What was it? Where is it? Where did it go?" I checked our depth. We were at eighty-five feet.

We kept on going, really slow. We were at ninety-eight feet. Kate started pointing at her pressure gauge. I checked my pressure. I still had two thousand pounds. Kate started signaling for us to turn around. David and I gave her the okay signal. We turned around and started back in.

The visibility was really bad now. We could only see about five feet at the most. We all got really close together. David started pointing for us to go at an angle. We turned a little and stayed together. The visibility started clearing up. We must have been going back in, through the dirt we kicked up going out. I checked my compass and pointed in. David gave me the okay signal. We turned and headed straight in. We kept going slowly, while sweeping with our dive lights. I could see something dark ahead of us. It was big and dark. I was getting really nervous then. I thought oh good! It's the bottom of the drop off.

We slowly went up to the drop off and went up it, then started along the sandy bottom. We were at thirty-three feet. Kate started pointing up. David and I gave her the okay signal. We got close together and started going up.

We were on the surface. We aired up our BC's, took our regulators out of our mouths and our mask off. I said, "Man, that was scary." Kate said, "Yeah, really scary." David said, "This is such a fun place to dive at." I said, "Man, is it dark out there!" Kate said, "It's really dark." We started kicking in.

We kicked in close, took our fins off, got out, walked over to the showers and rinsed off. Then we walked up to the cars, took our dive gear off and changed tanks. Kate said, "We need to do a shallow dive after that deep dive so our next dive we shouldn't go too deep." David and I said okay. Then David said to Kate, "We'll follow you. Go anywhere you want and we'll follow you." Kate said, "Okay."

We sat around talking. I checked my computer and said, "The computer is showing our maximum time for a hundred feet so we're okay to do our next dive when everyone is ready." David said, "I'm ready." Kate said, "Me too." I said, "Let's go."

We put our dive gear on, walked across the parking lot, down the steps and across the beach. I thought it was dark before but now it was really dark! Kate said, "Don't forget your BC." We all aired them up. I checked my compass. We turned on our dive lights, got in the water and put our fins on. We started kicking out. We kicked out a little way and Kate asked, "Do you guys want to go down here?" David and I both said okay. We put our masks on, our regulators in our mouths, got close together and slowly started letting the air out of our BC's. We were going down.

We were on the bottom. We gave each other the okay signal. We were at seventeen feet. I got on Kate's left side and David got on her right side. Kate pointed out. We started going slow along the sandy bottom. We could see the darkness from the drop off coming up. We went up to the edge of it and stopped. We started looking down it then Kate pointed out. David and I gave her the okay signal.

We started going down the drop off really slow. We got to the bottom of it then started going out. We were all sweeping with our dive lights but Kate kept looking at her gauges. We kept going slowly then Kate started pointing to our left and started turning in that direction. We were at seventy-one feet. David and I turned with her and stayed next to her.

We kept going, staying around seventy feet. We could see some dirt stirred up in front of us. I thought something is out here with us! We went through the dirt then I saw a bat ray swimming off toward the deeper water. I thought oh good it must have been bat rays. We kept slowly going, sweeping with our dive lights. Kate started pointing to the left again and started turning. David and I turned with her. We could see the bottom of the drop off coming up. We went up to it, then went up it.

We started going along the sandy bottom going in toward the shore. David started quickly shining his dive light back and forth on something. Kate and I shined our dive lights on it. It was a flounder about a foot and a half long. We went toward it. It swam off. We were at fifteen feet. Kate pointed up. David and I gave her the okay signal. We went up, aired up our BC's, took our regulators out of our mouths and our mask off. I said, "That dive wasn't as scary." Kate said, "Yeah that was a good dive." David didn't say anything. I knew he didn't like it because we went slow and didn't go very deep.

We kicked in close, took our fins off, got out, walked up to the showers and rinsed off. I said, "This water sure feels good after diving." Kate said, "It sure does." We walked up the steps and over to the cars. We took off our dive gear and wetsuits. We started packing everything in the cars. Kate said, "Thanks for letting me go with you guys." David and I said, "Your welcome." Kate got in her car and drove off.

David and I got in the car and started home. David said, "Let's stop and get a hamburger." I said, "Okay." We went through the drive through. I ordered for us then said, "Oh no my wallet is locked in the trunk!" David said, "That's okay. I'll get it."

We were on our way to David's house. David said, "I think we should stop using the chemsticks. Both of us keep a close eye on each other and we can always see the other one's dive light." I said, "I know. We know where each other is by the way we're sweeping with them." David said, "I can always tell when you're looking at something too because you stop sweeping with yours. The chemsticks are a waste of money for us but you should probably use them when you dive with girls." I started laughing and said, "I know you have to keep an eye on them." David said, "Isn't that the truth! I think from now on, you can dive with the girls. I have to dive with your sister and that's too much for me." I said, "Okay, I'll make the girls stay at home when we go diving from now on. Girls don't like to go fast, deep and at night for some reason." David said, "I know what a waste of diving."

We drove up to David's house. I said, "I'll air up the tanks." David said, "Okay." David unloaded his dive gear. I drove home, unloaded my dive gear and rinsed it off.

Saturday morning ...

I loaded my dive gear and my tanks in the car then drove to the dive shop. I carried the tanks in, sat them at the filling area and then walked to the front. Eddie was behind the counter. I said, "Can I get some air Eddie?" Eddie said, "You sure can." We walked to the back. Eddie started filling the tanks. I said, "I'm going diving with a girl named Kirsten at 10:00." Eddie said, "I wish I could go diving but I've got to work." I said, "I know what you mean." Eddie finished filling my tanks. We walked back to the front.

A young lady walked in. Eddie said, "Here she is now." It was a little before 10:00. I said, "Hi, I'm Lee." She said, "Hi, I'm Kirsten." I said, "Are you about ready to go?" Kirsten said, "I'm ready. Where would you like to go?" I said, "Is Redondo okay?" Kirsten said, "Sure." I said, "Let me load my tanks and I'll be ready. Do you want to go with me or meet down there?" Kirsten said, "I'll follow you down there if that's all right. I'm not coming back to the dive shop after diving." I said, "Okay. I'll load my tanks and drive around to the front." Kirsten said, "Okay. I'll be ready." I loaded my tanks and drove around to the front. Kirsten was sitting in her car. I drove past her and waved. She waved back and pulled up behind me. We were on our way to Redondo.

We drove into the parking lot and parked. It was crowded with students. I said, "Let's go check the surf." Kirsten said, "Okay." We walked over to the steps and looked at the waves. I said, "Good, they're small." Kirsten said, "Good."

We walked back to the cars, unloaded our dive gear and started putting it together. I asked, "You are going to live in a underwater laboratory?" Kirsten said, "Yes, I'm going to be doing research on the marine environment. That's why I need twenty-five dives in four weeks." I said, "Wow, you need to do a lot of diving. I've been diving a lot too." Kirsten said, "I'm so mad at the dive shop. I paid them to certify me, have a total of twenty-five dives done in four weeks with dive instructors and they haven't been getting me the dives." I said, "I'm not a dive instructor and I'm not working with the dive shop. I've just been doing a lot of diving." Kirsten said, "Thanks for diving with me. I really do appreciate it. Do you feel okay about going to a hundred feet? I haven't been able to find anyone to do a deep dive with me." I said, "I like doing deep dives. We can go to a hundred feet if you want." Kirsten said, "I've never done a deep dive before and I really do need to log one." I said, "That's no problem. We'll just go out to a hundred feet then turn around and come back in." Kirsten said, "Okay." I said, "There's a drop off out there that's almost even with the end of the pier. Let's go down the drop off then stop and make sure everything is okay. If everything is okay go out ten feet deeper and stop and make sure everything is okay. If everything is still okay, we'll keep doing that until we're at a hundred feet but if either one of us gets down to fifteen hundred pounds of air let's turn around and come back in no matter what depth we're at." Kirsten said, "Okay that's fine with me."

We opened our air up and checked our regulators. I said, "Are you about ready?" Kirsten said, "Yes." We put our wetsuits and dive gear on then walked across the parking lot, down the steps and across the beach. I pointed down the beach a little way and said, "Let's go in over there so we're out of the way of the students." Kirsten said, "Okay." We walked down the beach. I said, "Don't forget to air up your BC." We both aired them up. I wondered how she was going to act underwater. I had better keep a close eye on her since she's never been to a hundred feet before!

We got into the water, put our fins on and kicked out a little way from the shore. I said, "Are you ready to go down?" Kirsten said, "Yes." I set my compass. Kirsten set hers. We put our mask on and our regulators in our mouths. We slowly started letting the air out of our BC's and started going down.

We were on the bottom. We were sixteen feet deep. I gave Kirsten the okay signal. She gave it back. I checked my compass and pointed out. Kirsten gave me the okay signal. We started going along the bottom. She was staying right next to me on my right side.

We could see the drop off coming up. We went up to it, stopped and looked out over it. We checked our air and gave each other the okay signal. I pointed down the drop off. Kirsten gave me the okay signal. We started slowly going down the drop off. Kirsten seemed to be doing okay. She was looking around and staying right next to me.

We got to the bottom of the drop off and stopped. I gave her the okay signal. She gave it back. I pointed out. She gave me the okay signal. We started going. I was keeping a close eye on our depth.

We were at sixty feet. We stopped. She still seemed to be doing okay. I checked my air and she checked hers. I looked over at hers she had twenty six hundred pounds. I thought that's a good sign! She must not be too nervous or scared because she would be using it up faster.

I pointed out. She gave me the okay signal. We started going. We were looking around but not seeing much. We were at seventy feet so we stopped. I checked my air. Kirsten checked hers. I gave her the okay signal. She gave it back.

We started going again. We were looking around at the dirt bottom. We were at eighty feet so we stopped. I checked my air. Kirsten checked hers. I gave her the okay signal. She gave it back.

We started going again. We still weren't seeing anything. We were at ninety feet so we stopped. I checked my air. Kirsten checked hers. I thought she seems to be doing really good. I gave her the okay signal. She gave it back. We started going again.

We were at a hundred feet so we stopped. I checked my air. Kirsten checked hers. I gave her the okay signal. She gave it back. I looked over at her pressure gauge. She still had twenty two hundred pounds. I looked back at mine. I was down to nineteen hundred pounds. I thought wow! She's getting better air consumption than I am. I pointed to turn right and go for a little bit, then start in. I knew we would be in the dirt we stirred up if we didn't. Kirsten gave me the okay signal. We started going, staying at a hundred feet then I pointed to the right. Kirsten gave me the okay signal. We turned and started in. We were going slow, taking our time and looking around. We still weren't seeing anything.

We could see the bottom of the drop off coming up. We went up to it and stopped. I pointed to my power inflater so she would know to dump her air out of her BC on the way up. She grabbed hers and gave me the okay signal. We slowly started up the drop off.

We made it to the top then started going across the sandy bottom, going in. I pointed to the right so we would stay out of the way of the students. She gave me the okay signal. We turned and went a little way.

I pointed up. Kirsten gave me the okay signal. We started slowly going up. We were on the surface. Kirsten said, "That was fun!" I said, "Yeah, it was. I really like deep dives. You did really well." Kirsten said "Thank you." We started kicking in.

We kicked in close, took our fins off and got out. We walked up to the showers, rinsed off then walked up the steps and over to the cars. We took our dive gear off and changed tanks.

We sat around talking for a while then I checked my computer and said, "My computer is showing we can do our next dive now. So let me know when you're ready." Kirsten said, "Let me finish this bottle of water and I'll be ready." She was almost finished with it. Kirsten said, "Is it okay if we do a shallow dive and just stay up on top in the sandy area and look around?" I said, "Sure, we can dive any way that you want too."

We put our dive gear on, walked across the parking lot, down the steps and across the beach. I said, "Don't forget your BC." We both aired them up. We got in the water and put our fins on. I said, "Let's go down here." We were only about twenty feet from the shore. Kirsten said, "Okay." We put our mask on and our regulators in our mouths. We slowly let the air out of our BC's. We were on the bottom. We were twelve feet deep. I gave Kirsten the okay signal. She gave it back.

I pointed out. Kirsten gave me the okay signal. We started going out slowly, looking around at the sandy bottom. I looked to my left and saw a small crab walking along the sand. Kirsten saw me pointing at it. We went over to it and watched it.

We started going again. A small fish about six inches long swam past us. We kept going and could see the drop off up ahead of us. We went up close to it, turned left and started going along the top next to it. We were kicking along not seeing much. Kirsten pointed for us to turn to the left a little and veer away from the drop off. We turned and kept going slowly. We still weren't seeing much. We made another turn and started back toward where we came in at.

Kirsten started pointing. It was a small flounder about a foot long. We went toward it but it swam off. We kept kicking around and looking at the bottom. I checked my air. I was down to eight hundred pounds. I pointed toward the shore. Kirsten gave me the okay signal.

We started going in. We were getting really shallow. We could feel the little waves pulling and pushing us. I was close to the bottom but I could almost put my hand out of the water. I could see some legs swimming around in front of me. I stuck my head up out of the water and two little girls started screaming. It was two little girls and a little boy swimming. One of the little girls said, "You scared me. I thought you were a shark!" I said, "Sorry about that. You don't have to worry about sharks. We just checked and there's no sharks any where around here." The little girl said, "Oh good."

We took our fins off, got out, walked across the beach, up to the showers and rinsed off. We walked up the steps and over to the cars. We took our dive gear and wetsuits off and packed everything into our cars.

Kirsten said, "Will you sign my dive log?" I said, "Sure." Kirsten said, "Thanks for diving with me." I said, "You're welcome. In case I don't see you again before you leave, be careful at the underwater laboratory." Kirsten said, "Okay I will. Is there a store around to get a soda and chips?" I said, "Yeah just right down the street. Follow me." Kirsten said, "Okay."

We got in our cars. She followed me to the store and parked next to me. We went in. I got a soda and a candy bar. Kirsten got a soda and chips then said, "Here let me get it." I said, "You don't have to do that." Kirsten said, "I would be happy too." Kirsten paid for everything and said, "Thanks again."

We both got in our cars. I drove home, unloaded my dive gear, rinsed it off and put it up.

A little later …

David called and said, "The dive shop just called and said my computer, compass and console came in. Do you want to go with me and pick them up?" I said, "Yeah. I need to air up the tanks anyway."

David drove over to my house. We loaded all the tanks in David's truck, drove to the dive shop and parked. We carried the tanks in. Eddie was filling some tanks and said to David, "Let me start filling the tanks then I'll get your equipment." David said, "Okay." David, Eddie and I walked to the front of the dive shop. Eddie reached down behind the counter, picked it up and said, "Here you go." David said, "Thanks."

We walked back to the filling area. Eddie finished filling the tanks. We carried everything out to the truck. We were on our way back to my house. David said, "Do you want to go diving tomorrow?" I said, "Okay, I was looking at the book and there used to be an old pier to the left at Redondo, close to that rock jetty, that is at the far end of the beach. It was called Redondo Pier #3. There's supposed to be some pillars still from it underwater. How about checking it out?" David said, "Okay, let's do one dive there before dark. If we like it, we can do the next one after dark." I said, "Okay, sounds good to me." David drove me home. We unloaded the tanks and put them up then David went home.

Sunday evening …

David called and said, "I got everything mounted in the console. Everything fit perfectly and it was easy." I said, "Good, I didn't think it would be very hard." David asked, "Are you about ready." I said, "I'm ready." David said, "I'll be right over."

I started loading my dive gear and the tanks in the car. David drove up and loaded his dive gear. We were on our way to Redondo Pier #3. David said, "Kate sure did run out of air fast." I said, "I think she's real nervous on deep dives - especially deep dives at night! I thought I used my air up faster then anyone but she uses way more than I do." David said, "Kate runs out of air fast and Deb is slow, looking at every little thing. It's so much fun when it's just me and you. We get out there, deep, in the middle of the night." I said, "I like diving both ways but it definitely is more exciting the way we dive."

David said, "Are we stopping and getting taco's? They make me burp." I said, "Yeah." We drove through the Mexican food dive through and picked up our food. David started looking at the book then said, "It looks like we'll have to park in the street. It doesn't show any parking lots there. It doesn't look like we'll be able to get as deep as we do at Redondo either." I said, "I know, but it's suppose to still have some of the pilings from the old pier that will be neat to look at."

We started getting close. There were a lot of condos and we could only park on the street. We looked for a parking spot but couldn't find any. David said, "Over there. That car is leaving." I said, "Okay." I hurried up, drove over and parked. We sat in the car and ate.

We got out, unloaded our dive gear and put it together behind the car, in between my car and the car behind us. We didn't have much room. We started putting our wetsuits on. We were hopping back and forth, out into the street some. David said, "I hope we don't get run over." I said, "Me too." We finished putting our wetsuits on then put our dive gear on.

We started walking. It felt like we were walking down a sidewalk in the middle of town. David said, "I feel kind of stupid walking down the sidewalk with a wetsuit and dive gear on." I said, "Me too." David said, "I think we walk past these condos then turn right." I said, "I wish we could have parked a little closer." David said, "Me too."

We kept walking and turned at the corner. We finally made it to the beach and started walking in front of one of the big condo buildings. David said, "It's a long walk to this beach. I'm worn out now." I said, "So am I." David said, "The picture in the book shows the pilings are out in front of that condo building" he started pointing at the next building. We walked toward the water in front of the condo. I said, "I think they're less then sixty feet deep." David said, "Yeah. They're not very deep. Are you going to let me navigate with my new compass?" I said, "It's all yours."

We were close to the water. We aired up our BC's, got in, put our fins on and started kicking out. We kicked out a little way then David said, "I think we should go down here and check it out." I said, "Okay." We put our mask on, our regulators in our mouths and started letting the air out of our BC's. We were going down, slowly.

We were on the bottom. We were twenty feet deep. David started pointing out. I gave him the okay signal. We started going along the bottom. I was staying next to David thinking how nice it was not to have to worry about where we're at or getting lost. I started looking around. We were going fast but we weren't getting very deep. We weren't seeing anything either. David starting pointing for us to veer off to the right. I stayed next to him. We were still going along, fast. David started pointing at something to his side. I looked over there. It was one of the pilings. I thought oh my gosh! That's neat looking, it's completely pink. Nothing out there had much color except for this pink piling standing up about eight feet tall. It was completely covered with little pink sea anemones. We went up to it and went around it, looking at it.

We looked at it for awhile then David started pointing out toward the deep water. I gave him the okay signal. We started going out. We were going real fast. I was still thinking how nice it was, not having to navigate and worry about anything. I checked my air. I still had eighteen hundred pounds. We kept going. We were at eighty-five feet. David started pointing for us to turn to the right then start back in. I thought I wonder why he want's to go back in so early? I gave him the okay signal.

We turned to the right and went a little way, then turned and started back in. We still weren't seeing anything. We kept going in, fast.

We were at fourteen feet. David starting pointing up. I gave him the okay signal. We went up, aired up our BC's, took our regulators out of our mouths and our mask off. I asked, "How come you came back in so early?" David said, "So early! I was down to fourteen hundred pounds when we turned around." I said, "Really? I still had eighteen hundred pounds. You mean that I got better air consumption then you did? It must have been because you were navigating. That's funny." David said, "That is."

We kicked in close, took our fins off and got out. The sun was just starting to go down. David said, "I don't like this place very much." I said, "I don't either." David said, "Let's go do some real diving at our favorite dive spot." I said, "Okay." We walked across the beach, down the sidewalk and back to the car. We took our dive gear off. I said, "I'm leaving my wetsuit on." David said, "I will too." We loaded our dive gear in the car.

We were driving over to the Redondo parking lot. I said, "I feel kind of stupid driving a car wearing a wet wetsuit." David said, "Yeah, you look pretty stupid driving like that but I feel stupid being a passenger wearing a wet wetsuit." We drove into the parking lot and parked. We got out, unloaded our dive gear and changed tanks.

David asked, "How is our time looking?" I looked at my computer and said, "It looks like we still have a little while to go." David said, "That's what I thought. I was double-checking my computer. It looks like it's going to be nice and dark when we go in." I said, "Yeah. It's already pretty dark."

A few minutes later David said, "My computer is showing the maximum time for a hundred feet." I said, "Mine is too. I'm ready when you are." David said, "Let's go." We put our dive gear on, walked across the parking lot, down the steps and across the beach to the water. David said, "I'm not turning my dive light on until we're ready to go down." I said, "Okay I won't either." We aired up our BC's, got in, put our fins on and started kicking out. David looked up at the moon and said, "It's a full moon and it sure is bright." I said, "It sure is." David said, "The moon is bright and look at all the lights that are on" he was looking toward the beach. I looked down into the water and said, "Yeah it's lit up pretty good isn't it. But look how dark the water is." David said, "It is dark. I sure like it here. It's easy to park, no crowd and good diving."

David looked toward the pier and said, "I think we're close. Are you ready?" I said, "I'm ready." David started checking his compass. I said, "Good, you're navigating again." David said, "Yeah. I'll navigate." We turned on our dive lights, put our mask on, our regulators in our mouths and started letting the air out of our BC's. We were going down, slowly.

We were on the bottom. We were at thirty-five feet. David checked his compass and pointed out. I gave him the okay signal. We started going out at our normal fast pace. We came up to the top of the drop off and stopped. David pointed out. I gave him the okay signal. We went down the drop off, got to the bottom of it and kept going, not slowing down any.

We were going fast, sweeping with our dive lights. I could see something coming up to my left. It was bright orange. I started shining my dive light on it steady, not sweeping anymore. David noticed I was looking at something and started shining his dive light on it. We turned and kicked over to it. It's a construction cone they use to put on the road at construction sights. I thought how in the world did this get down here? I picked it up and looked in it. Something is in it. I looked down at it then stuck my hand into the cone and grabbed it. I pulled it out. It was a small octopus. I got a good grip on it then started quickly moving it up and down and side to side really fast trying to get it mad. It was inking all over the place. I pointed it at David and let it go. It quickly swam off away from both of us, really fast. I looked at David and raised my shoulders and eyebrows up like oh well.

We started going out again at our fast pace. We were at a hundred and nineteen feet. David started pointing for us to turn to the right. We turned and started going fast again. After a little way, David started pointing to the right again. We turned and started back in. We were sweeping with our dive lights and going at our normal fast pace. I noticed David wasn't sweeping with his dive light. I quickly looked over at what he was looking at. We slowed down and went toward it. It was something brown moving on the dirt, crawling. We kept looking at it and slowly went close to it. We were a few feet from it. It was some kind of crab, a big crab that looked like a giant spider. It was scary looking. It was about the size of a cat. It had long skinny legs and small claws. It was slowly crawling away from us. We watched it crawl away. David started pointing in. I gave him the okay signal.

We were going along fast. We could see the bottom of the drop off coming up. We went up to it, went up it then started going in along the sandy bottom. I was down to four hundred pounds of air. I pointed my dive light in front of David and quickly moved it back and forth. David looked at me. I pointed up. David gave me the okay signal.

We went up, aired up our BC's, took our regulators out of our mouths and our mask off. I said, "Man that was fun. That octopus and that crab thing were really neat." David said, "What were you doing with that octopus?" I said, "Scott told me that he heard if you grab an octopus and shake it up then point it at your dive buddy it'll quickly swim to them and stick onto them. That one must have gotten confused." David said, "Oh! I thought you were molesting it or something." I started laughing and said, "Oh my gosh! That's funny."

We kicked in close, took our fins off and got out. We walked over to the showers, rinsed off, walked up the steps to the car and started taking our dive gear off. David said, "We went to a hundred and nineteen feet on this dive and eighty five feet on our first one. You're always suppose to do your shallow dive first right?" I said, "Yeah that's right." We both started laughing. We finished taking our dive gear and wetsuits off. We loaded everything in the car. We were on our way home.

David said, "I'm hungry let's eat." I said, "Oh no!" David said, "Let me guess … the trunk." I said, "I tried to remember it this time. Let me stop and get it." David said, "I'll get it since you're always getting the air." I said, "Yeah, but that's only four dollars. You're getting ripped off." David said, "It's not enough to worry about." We drove through the drive through and got hamburgers, then drove to my house. We started unloading our dive gear and the tanks. David loaded his dive gear in his truck and went home.

I rinsed off my dive gear, put it up then went in to look in my book that I had bought from the dive shop with a lot of pictures of fish and sea animals in it. I found that crab and started reading about it. I waited a few minutes for David to get home then I called him. I said, "That crab was a sheep crab. It can stick stuff that it finds onto its body." David said, "That's pretty weird." I said, "It is and it sure was scary looking too."

Monday …

I loaded the tanks in the car, drove to the dive shop, carried them in and put them at the filling area. Ron walked up and said, "Hello. Do you need a little air?" I said, "Yeah, whenever you get a chance." Ron aired them up. I said, "Thanks Ron." I carried the tanks out to the car and drove home.

I called Deb and said, "I signed up to go on a three day boat trip to the Santa Barbara Channel Islands and also a trip to an underwater dive park at Catalina. You can't swim at the dive park, only dive. Do you want to go?" Deb said, "Oh man! That sounds like fun but I better not go this time. I'll try to go next time." I said, "Okay." Deb said, "We're still going diving tomorrow, right." I said, "Yeah." Deb said, "Let's go to Redondo tomorrow evening and do a day dive and a night dive." I said, "Okay."

Tuesday evening …

Deb called and said, "Let's go." I said, "Okay let me load my dive gear and I'll be over." I loaded the tanks and dive gear in the car then drove to Deb's house. Deb loaded her dive gear.

We were on our way to Redondo. I said, "Guess who came over yesterday evening?" Deb said, "Who?" I said, "Lee, they moved back down here. I sure didn't like taking him home though." Deb said, "Why not?" I said, "Something just didn't seem right." Deb said, "We'll that's good that they moved back down here anyway."

I said, "Are you hungry? David and I have been stopping and getting tacos on the way. David says they make him burp." Deb said, "Yeah. Go ahead and stop. I'm hungry but I don't know about the burping part. I hope we see something good like that school of fish." I said, "David and I saw an octopus and a sheep crab last time. Wait until you see a sheep crab. They're almost as big as a cat and they look like a giant spider. They take stuff off the bottom and stick it onto themselves." Deb said, "Those sound neat."

We drove through the drive through and got taco's and sodas then drove to the parking lot, parked and started eating. Deb said, "On that boat trip you're going on, where do you sleep?" I said, "There are bunks on the boat." Deb said, "I don't think I could sleep very well on a boat." I said, "I know I'm kind of worried about that too." Deb said, "I bet it's going to be fun though anyway." I said, "I hope so." We finished eating.

We walked over and looked at the waves. Deb said, "Good. Small, just like I like them." I said, "Me too." We walked back to the car, unloaded our dive gear and started putting it together. I said, "It's funny when I dive with you we go slow and take our time but when I dive with David we go really fast." Deb said, "David goes too fast for me. I can barely keep up with him." I said, "I know he does like to go fast." Deb said, "I like to look at everything and have a fun dive." I said, "It's really fun here but at night it's a little scary sometimes. Sometimes I feel like something is out there with us." Deb remarked, "You're always scared."

We finished putting our dive gear together and started putting our wetsuits on. Deb said, "What's our dive plan?" I said, "Let's kick out close to the end of the pier. That way, we will be close to the edge of the drop off. Then go out until one of us is down to fifteen hundred pounds but let's not go past a hundred and thirty feet." Deb said, "Okay."

We put our dive gear on, walked across the parking lot, down the steps then across the beach to the water. I said, "Don't forget to air up your BC." We both aired them up. We got into the water, put our fins on and started kicking out.

I looked down at the pier. We were almost even with the end of it. I said, "This looks good to me." Deb said, "Me too. Let's go." We put our mask on, our regulators in our mouths and started letting the air out of our BC's. We were going down, slowly.

We were on the bottom. We were right next to the edge of the drop off. I thought man! We almost went out too far and went down into the deep water! I gave Deb the okay signal. She gave it back. I pointed down the drop off. Deb gave me the okay signal. We started going down the drop off. We got to the bottom of it and slowly started going out.

We were going out, slow, not seeing too much. We were looking around. I could see something crawling on the bottom in front of us. Deb was looking at it too. We went toward it, it was a sheep crab. We went over to it and stopped to really look at it close-up. We kept looking at it. Deb started going even closer to it and was just staring at it, moving her head side to side while getting a real close and good look at it. Like what in the world is this creature. We watched it for a little while then I pointed out toward the deep water. Deb gave me the okay signal.

We were going really slow just looking around. I looked down and checked my compass then looked back up. Deb was pointing at something ahead of us. It was something with a big head pointed at us. We started going toward it. All of a sudden it started swimming off, along with two other ones that were next to it. It was three bat rays! We stopped to watch them. They stirred up the dirt. We started going and went straight through the dirty water.

I checked my air. I was down to fifteen hundred pounds. We were at a hundred and twenty two feet. I signaled to Deb for us to start back in. Deb gave me the okay signal. We turned right and went a little way then turned right again and started in. We were going in slow, looking around.

We could see the bottom of the drop off coming up. We went up to it and started up it. I checked my air and thought man, I'm getting low on air. I'm down to four hundred pounds. We were almost at the top of the drop off. I signaled to Deb for us to go straight up. She gave me the okay signal.

We went up, aired up our BC's, took off our regulators out of our mouths and our mask off. Deb said, "That crab was neat and so were those bat rays! This is a neat place to dive but I bet it is a little scary out there at night. On our night dive, let's either go down the drop off staying around the bottom of it or on the drop off and look at it." I said, "That's fine with me."

We kicked in close, took our fins off and got out. We walked over to the showers, rinsed off, walked up the steps and over to the car. We took our dive gear off and changed tanks.

After a little while Deb said, "The sun is almost completely down now. Are you about ready?" I said, "Let me check the computer." I looked at it and said, "Yeah. We're ready." Deb said, "Since we're not going deep, let's just get in, go down right away and look around in the shallow water too." I said, "Okay."

We cracked our chemsticks and tied them to our tanks. I said, "David and I quit using chemsticks but we'll use them just to be safe." Deb said, "That sounds like David." We put our dive gear on, walked across the parking lot, down the steps and across the beach. We aired up our BC's, turned on our dive lights, got in and put our fins on. Deb said, "Let's go down." I said, "Okay." We were so shallow my fins were hitting the bottom.

We put our mask on, our regulators in our mouths and let the air out of our BC's. We were only five feet deep. I pointed out. Deb gave me the okay signal. We started slowly going along the bottom. I noticed how the sandy bottom had small hills and valleys as we were going out. The waves must have caused them. I thought it would be easy to not get lost in the sandy area. If we were going across the small hills and valleys while equalizing our ears, then we must be going out. I quit looking at my compass and kept watching the bottom. I signaled to Deb and started pointing at the hills and valleys then at my compass. She gave me the blank look. I thought oh well. I'll tell her later. I shook my head, never mind and pointed out.

We slowly kept going while sweeping with our dive lights. I saw a little reflection to my left and up about four or five feet. I stopped and started shining my dive light on it. I started looking at it. I looked over at Deb. She was looking at it too. It's a small orange crab with two claws swimming sideways. It's swimming through the water. I thought it must have gone to the surface for air or something. I looked at Deb. She looked at me. I shrugged my shoulders and pointed out. We left it alone and started going.

I could see the dark area coming up from the drop off. We went up to it, stopped and looked down it. It was dark. Real dark. It looked a lot scarier with Deb than it did with David. We kept looking down it. Deb started pointing down it. I took a big breath and gave her the okay signal. We started slowly going down it.

We got to the bottom of the drop off and started going out. I pointed to our left to turn and go along next to the bottom of the drop off. Deb gave me the okay signal. We turned and kept going. Deb was closest to the drop off and I was on the open ocean side. We started going, looking at the bottom of the drop off and shining our dive lights up on it. We weren't seeing much.

Deb gave me a hand signal to follow her. I gave her the okay signal. She went about half way up the drop off then started going back in the opposite direction. We kept going, slowly, looking at the side of the drop off. Every now and then we would see some small schools of fish that looked like little freshwater guppies. Deb and I would shine our dive lights at them and point at them.

I checked my air. I was down to nine hundred pounds. I pointed for us to go up to the top of the drop off. Deb gave me the okay signal. We turned, went up to the top of the drop off and then slowly started going in. I saw a flounder not too far in front of us. I shined my dive light on it then quickly moved it back and forth to get Deb's attention. She shined hers on it. We went over to it. It was only about six inches long. It was staying still. We looked at it then I poked at it. It started swimming off. Deb and I started chasing it. We were going fast but it was faster then we were and it gradually swam away from us. I checked my air. I was down to four hundred pounds. We were at twenty-two feet. I pointed up to Deb. She gave me the okay signal. We went up, aired up our BC's, took our regulators out of our mouths and our mask off.

Deb said, "That's fun but it did seem dark." I said, "It's fun but it's scary." We kicked in close, took our fins off, got out, walked to the showers and rinsed off. We walked up to the car and took our dive gear off. I asked Deb if she was hungry. She said she was. I said, "How about a hamburger?" Deb said, "Okay." I said, "I usually forget my money in the trunk. I better put it in the car now or I'll forget it again." We loaded everything in the car, drove through, got our hamburgers and started driving to Deb's house. Deb asked, "When are we going diving next?" I said, "When do you want to go?" Deb said, "I can't go until next week. How about Thursday?" I said, "That should be okay." We drove up to Deb's house. Deb unloaded her dive gear. I drove home, unloaded mine, rinsed it off and put it up.

Chapter 5

You're Privileged to See a Dangerous Shark

Wednesday …

I loaded the tanks in the car, drove to the dive shop, carried them in and put them at the filling area. I walked up to the front. Eddie was talking to a guy. I heard Eddie say to him, "I'll be right back." Eddie started walking to the back and said, "Hello Lee. Do you need some air?" I said, "Hello Eddie. Yeah, when you get a chance." Eddie said, "I can get them now." Eddie filled my tanks. I said, "Thanks Eddie" and loaded them in the car and drove home.

Thursday …

David called and said, "Let's go diving tonight." I said, "I can't tonight let's go tomorrow night." David said, "Okay." I said, "I'm going to get my tires balanced tomorrow after work. The steering wheel has been bouncing back and forth a little when I get on the freeway. I'll be over as soon as they get finished with them. It shouldn't take too long." David said, "Okay."

Friday afternoon …

I drove home from work, loaded all the dive gear in the car and drove to the tire shop. The tire shop was only a couple of blocks from David's house. I parked in front of one of their garages and walked inside. I told the manager what was wrong with the car.

They drove the car into the garage and started working on it. I sat down and looked at a couple of magazines then I started walking around looking at the tire stuff. I noticed on the door that they closed at 5:00. It was five minutes to 5:00. I had been there over an hour. I thought I hope they get them done in time. The manager walked out to the garage then walked back in and said, "They're finished." I said, "Oh good."

I walked over to the counter. He told me how much it cost. I started filling out the check. I said, "Do you know what the date is?" He said, "Yeah, the 13th, Friday the 13th". I said, "Oh, you're kidding." He said, "No, all day long" and acted like it hadn't been a very good day. I filled out the check and gave it to him. He gave me the keys. I walked out to the car, got in it and drove to David's house. David loaded his dive gear.

We were going down the street toward the freeway. We were going forty-m.p.h. I looked at David and said, "It's not right, it seems even worse than before!" David said, "Do you want to take it back?" I said, "They closed at 5:00, ten minutes ago. Let's see what happens." I drove up the freeway on ramp and got on the freeway. I was in the slow lane doing fifty. The steering wheel was bouncing back and forth so bad I could barely hold onto it. I said, "This is bad! I can't believe they messed them up this bad!" David said, "Do you want to go in my truck?" I said, "I need to drive to work tomorrow so we should probably try to get it fixed. I know a department store that does tires and they are close. Let's go there." David said, "Okay."

We were on our way to the department store. David asked, "Do you want to stop and get something to eat? That way we can eat while they're working on it." I said, "I don't know of any place that is close, do you?" David said, "No, I can't think of any."

We were getting close to the department store. I said, "Oh by the way, guess who has been coming over?" David said, "Who." I said, "Lee. They moved back down here and he's been calling me to come get him after school." David said, "Good. I'm glad you're getting to see him." I said, "Me too."

We drove into the parking lot and parked next to the garage. The manager walked up to the car. I said, "My tires needed balanced so I took the car to a tire shop. They just got finished balancing them and then they closed at 5:00. I got on the freeway and could barely go fifty-m.p.h. the steering wheel was bouncing so bad. They did something wrong." The manager said, "We'll take a look at them."

David and I walked inside and started looking around. After awhile the manager came in and said, "Those tires were so much out of balance. They were out of balance more then any tires I have ever seen. We balanced them and you're ready to go." I said, "Thanks! I don't think I'll ever use that tire shop again." I filled out the check, looked at David and said, "This didn't happen because its Friday the 13^{th,} did it?" David said, "I don't think so."

David and I went out and got in the car. We were on our way to the freeway. David said, "I saw a sign at the parking lot saying it closes at 10:00. We're going to have to hurry now if we're going to do two dives before 10:00." I said, "Okay. I'll hurry it up." We drove up and got on the freeway. We were going seventy five-mph. I said, "Man, they did a good job. I don't think it's ever driven this smooth."

We were getting close to the Mexican fast food restaurant. I said, "We're getting taco's … right?" David said, "Yeah." I said, "I think I want a burrito and two taco's this time." David said, "I want the usual three tacos."

We drove through the drive through. I ordered five tacos, one burrito, a diet soda and a regular soda. They said, "Please drive up." We waited in line behind two cars in front of us. David said, "Since we're running late, what do you say we get there, eat without looking at the surf, hurry up, get the dive gear ready, put it on, get in the water, go down right away, go out fast and burn up that tank of air. Then get out and have our surface interval until 9:00. Then do our last dive and be back a little before 10:00 so we can be out of the parking lot by 10:00." I said, "Okay, Let's eat, hurry up and go out as fast as we can. You going to navigate?" David said, "Yeah."

We drove up to the drive through window. The girl at the window said, "That will be six dollars and sixty six cents please." I said to her, "Oh my gosh! You're kidding!" She said, "No, six dollars and sixty six cents." I said, "I can't believe its six dollars and sixty six cents on Friday the 13th." She gave me a strange look like I was some kind of weirdo. I handed her the money. She gave us the food.

We were on our way. David said, "I'm going to start eating now so I'll be ready when we get there." I said, "That's a good idea. Hand me mine. I'll eat while I'm driving." We started eating. I was trying to eat while hurrying up and driving. We finished eating.

We drove into the parking lot and parked. It was really dark. We quickly got out, unloaded the dive gear and started putting it together. A lone diver was walking past us. David and I looked up at him. He had a spear gun. David said, "Hi, how you doing?" The diver said, "Good, and you?" David said, "A little late but other than that good." The diver said, "I'll see you out there" as he walked past us. David and I kept hurrying. We started putting our wetsuits on. We weren't paying attention to each other, just hurrying as fast as we could. David said, "Can you get my hood?" I quickly went over and helped him with it. We put our dive gear on. We were ready.

We quickly walked across the parking lot, down the steps and started walking across the beach. David said, "Air up your BC." We both aired them up as we were walking fast. We turned on our dive lights. I said, "Get in, go down, go out fast." David said, "Yeah." We walked straight into the water not slowing down any. We put our fins on, our mask on, put our regulators in our mouths and let the air out of BC's. We were on the bottom. We were about five feet deep. We didn't give the okay signal or slow down any. We just started going out really fast.

We kept going out really fast. We could see the drop off coming up and it was dark, like usual. We went up to it and straight over it as fast as we could go, without slowing down at all. We were going down the drop off. We were kicking as fast as we could. We got to the bottom of the drop off and started going out, still going as fast as we could.

We were sweeping with our dive lights and going really fast. We could see something coming up ahead of us on the bottom. We both started shining our dive lights on it. It was a two-foot long dead fish. We were both shining our dive lights on it but not slowing down any. It only had a head and a tail and the middle was only bones. I thought we've never seen a dead fish like that and come to think of it, we've never seen a live one that size either. We both kept looking at it as we went over it. We weren't slowing down any, we were still going as fast as we could and sweeping with our dive lights.

We could barely see a dive light straight in front of us. I thought it must be that diver with the spear gun. David started pointing to the left a little. We both veered to the left, still not slowing down at all. We kept going as fast as we could. We were going past the other diver. It looked like he was about fifteen feet away from us. The visibility wasn't the greatest and we could just barely see his dive light. We kept going fast. We were kicking, going fast, sweeping with our dive lights, go, go, go. I have never gone this fast, this far before.

Wait, wait, wait there's something in front of us. It's big and dark, straight in front of us. About ten feet from us, it's really big. We're going to run into it! Stop, stop, stop! I quit kicking and coasted straight toward it. I wasn't slowing down very fast. I started back paddling with my arms. I felt like I was a train that couldn't stop.

We finally stopped and started staring at it. We were five feet from it. I thought oh my gosh this is a sharks tail, a sharks tail, I can't believe it, oh my gosh, I'm dead, I'm dead! I shined my dive light to my left and all the way to the top of the tail then back down to in front of me then to the right toward its head. I couldn't see it's head, it was too long. I shined my dive light back to the tail and up it again. I kept thinking I'm dead. I'm dead! The shark wasn't moving and I wasn't either.

Wait … what's going on? David's moving. What's he doing? David started slowly moving closer toward it. I thought it must not be as bad as I think. It must not be dangerous or David wouldn't go toward it. David knows what he's doing.

We must be safe. We're okay. I started watching David. He was shining his dive light on it and went up to it. He was only two feet from it. He was shining his dive light up and down it and back and forth on it. He slowly turned to the right and started going along side of it, toward its head. He was shining his dive light up and down it looking closely at it. I was looking at David and his tank. The shark was so thick that it was a lot higher than David's tank and a lot lower then David's stomach. I thought man this shark is big! David kept going along beside it, looking at it. I could see David's head but I couldn't see the shark's head. I kept thinking, "Man, this shark is big!" David was still shining his dive light up and down it and looking closely at it. It still hadn't moved any. I was staying still, shining my dive light back and forth, looking at its tail and toward its head.

David jerked back away from it and started quickly swimming backwards with his hands and moving away from it. I thought oh no, I'm dead, I'm dead! The big tail started moving back and forth like a big door swinging side to side. I started panicking and thinking, "I'm dead, I'm dead." The huge tail was swinging back and forth as it went past me. The shark was going to my right and veering to its right. We kept shining our dive lights on it as it faded out of sight. I thought it's veering to its right so it can turn around to come back and get us.

I quickly rolled over on my back and started kicking away from the direction it went in as fast as I could. I was shining my dive light between my fins looking for it thinking it would be coming back after us. I thought go, go, go! Kick, kick, kick! He's coming back after us. We're dead. We're dead! Air bubbles were everywhere! I'm still on my back looking between my fins. I could see David on my right side. I thought I hope David's watching in front of us. I'm watching behind us. I shined my dive light to the sides then back between my fins, all the while thinking, go, go, go, kick, kick, kick! I thought just go as fast as I can and don't slow down any. I shined my dive light to the sides again then back between my fins, go, go, go!

Oh no! He's got me, he's got me, he's got my leg. I can't move my leg. He's got my leg! Dirt was stirred up really bad. I couldn't see anything I could feel him pulling at my leg. Oh no! Here he is next to me! What? Wait a minute! That isn't the shark! It's the bottom of the drop off! I ran into the drop off! I haven't been bitten, it's the bottom of the drop off! I'm okay! Go, go, go get up the drop off! I turned over onto my stomach and started up the drop off as fast as I could go. There's David. He's okay! Go, go, go! We were kicking as fast as we could. We quickly went to the top of the drop off and over it. We were going in as fast as we could.

Go, go, go! I'm thinking don't stop! David keep kicking! We're kicking as fast as we can. Go, go, go! Don't slow down any! We were getting shallower and shallower I'm not sure how deep we are but we're getting close. I can see the surface. Yeah! We're real close. We went up, quickly took our fins off. I'm still thinking hurry, hurry, hurry! Get out, get out! We got out of the water, took our regulators out of our mouths and our mask off.

I looked at David and said, "We're alive, we're alive!" We turned around and started looking out toward the water. David said, "I can't believe how big it was." I said, "I can't either! It was huge! Why in the world did you go up to it and get as close as you did? You were only about two feet from it." David said, "At first I thought it was a grouper. So I went up to it and started looking at it. But when I got to the head. I shined my dive light into its eye. That's when I realized it was a shark. Its eye was as big as a softball! It was sleeping and when I shined my dive light into its eye, I woke it up and then it took off!

I said, "Oh my gosh! That was so scary! I thought it had my leg but I must have stuck it in the mud on the drop off some way. I wasn't watching where we were going and ran into the drop off and thought it was the shark. Oh know! That diver with the spear gun. When the shark took off it went straight toward him." David said, "That's right it did." We both stood on the beach looking at the dark water and didn't say anything.

We kept looking at the water. David said, "There he is over there, coming in!" He was out in the water about a hundred feet from shore down the beach a little way. We quickly walked toward where he was coming in at.

He was getting close to shore. I yelled, "Did you see it." He yelled back "What?" I waited for him to get closer. He started getting out. I said, "It was a huge shark. We scared it and it took off headed straight toward you." He said, "No, I didn't see it! What kind was it?" I said, "I don't know but its body was really thick and it was so long I couldn't see its head." David said, "It might have been a white shark." The diver said, "I've heard there's a six gill shark around here. Maybe that was it." I said, "What ever it was it was big!"

David and I walked toward the showers. David said, "Didn't you see my signal?" I said, "What signal?" David said, "The okay signal I was giving you." I said, "Okay, signal for what?" David said, "I was trying to tell you I was okay so we could keep diving." I said, "What? Keep diving? I'm never going out there again! Okay signal! Keep diving! Oh my god, keep diving! I can't believe it! The last thing I was looking for was an okay signal. I was only thinking, get out of this water and as fast as I could!"

We walked up to the showers, rinsed off and started walking back to the car. We were walking past one of the fences that was made of wood. I stopped and remarked, "Look at these posts." I stretched my arms out from one post toward the other post. Then said, "From my finger on this hand to my finger on my other hand is six feet. These posts must be about ten feet apart - if that's ten feet, how long do you think it was?" David started pointing about four feet past the first ten-foot post then said, "It was well over ten feet." I said, "I never even saw the head of it, it was so long." David said, "I'll never forget that eye."

We walked to the car, took our dive gear off and started talking about how scary it was. A few minutes later David said, "Are you about ready to change tanks?" I said, "What for?" David said, "For our next dive." I said, "What next dive? I'm not ever getting back in that water!" David said, "You mean you're going to waste your other tank of air?" I said, "Yeah." David said, "You mean your going to waste your other tank of air when the diving is perfect. That doesn't sound like you." I said, "I'm not ever going back in that shark infested water!"

David looked at his dive computer and said, "That dive was only for ten minutes and it was to *91 FEET*." We started laughing. I said, "It sure wasn't a very long dive, was it? I can't believe all of that happened in ten minutes." David said, "That was an exciting ten minutes." I said, "It sure was. Let's go to Deb's. She probably has a book on sharks." David said, "Okay." We took our wetsuits off and loaded everything in the car.

We drove to Deb and Scott's house. I started ringing the doorbell. Deb came to the door. I said, "You'll never believe what we just saw." Deb said, "What?" I said, "A shark, a huge shark at Redondo. Do you have any shark books? We want to see what kind it was." Deb said, "I've mostly got biology books. We can look but I doubt if I have one." David and I followed Deb.

We started looking at some books. As we were looking through them David said, "It was like running into the side of a station wagon, it was so big." I said, "Yeah and you went up to it." Deb said, "How close did you get?" I said, "I was five feet from it and David was two feet from it. He was looking it over as he was going down the side of it." Deb said, "That sounds scary." I said, "I can't believe it, it's Friday the 13th, we had car trouble, our Mexican food order was six dollars and sixty six cents then we almost got eaten by a shark!" Deb said, "That is pretty weird." I said, "It was so big I could have laid in it and had plenty of room to move around."

We kept looking at the books. Deb said, "Here are some sharks." We started looking at them. David said, "The body was thick like this white shark." I said,

"Yeah and this mako. It wasn't thin like this blue shark." David said, "I think it was a white shark." I said, "I do too." We sat and talked to Deb for awhile, then we got in the car and started driving to David's house. David said, "I can't go diving until next Sunday. You want to go then?" I said, "Okay, but I might want to do day dives." David said, "Okay." We drove up to David's house. David unloaded his dive gear. I drove home, unloaded mine, rinsed it off and put it up.

Saturday evening …

I started looking at a magazine that had dive equipment in it. It had a big dive light like David's and also a dive knife that I liked. I thought I'll see if the dive shop has them so I won't have to order them.

I loaded the two empty tanks in the car and drove to the dive shop. I carried the tanks in, put them at the filling area and walked to the front. Eddie said, "Hello." I said, "Hello, can I get some air. I want to look at your dive lights and dive knives too. David and I saw a big shark at Redondo last night. My dive light is way too small. I need a big one." Eddie said, "How big was the shark?" I said, "It was at least ten feet long." Eddie asked "What kind?" I said, "We think it was a white shark. It had a big thick body." Eddie said, "I've heard there's sharks at Redondo. Help yourself. I'll go air up your tanks." I said, "Thanks, Eddie." I started looking at the dive lights and dive knives. After a little while Eddie walked up. I said, "Are these the biggest dive lights you have?" Eddie said, "Yes we're sold out of the real big ones but we should be getting some in soon." I said, "That's okay. I'll let you know if I need one." I loaded the tanks in the car and drove home.

I called the company that sent me the catalog, ordered the dive light and dive knife. I called David and said, "I just ordered the biggest dive light I could find. It's like yours." David said, "I really like mine." I said, "I ordered a dive knife too so now we'll both have dive knives. They said it'll take a few days to get them." David said, "Good. Hopefully you'll get them before our next dive." I said, "I think I will."

I called Kate and asked, "Are you ready to go to the Channel Islands?" Kate said, "I'm ready." I said, "Do you want me to pick you up in the morning?" Kate said, "I can meet you at your house. It will be out of your way to come out here and pick me up." I said, "Okay." Kate said, "I'll call you in the morning before I leave."

Very early Sunday morning …

I got up and started loading my dive gear. Kate called and said, "I'm leaving now." I said, "Okay. I'll see you in a little bit." I finished loading all my dive gear in the car. Kate drove up and parked. She loaded her dive gear in the car.

We were on our way to Santa Barbara. I said, "You'll never believe what David and I saw Friday night." Kate said, "What?" I said, "A shark! A big shark at Redondo." Kate said, "How big?" I said, "It was at least ten feet long." Kate said, "No!" I said, "It scared me so bad. I wouldn't even do the second dive with David." Kate said, "I've never seen anything that big."

We kept driving. Kate said, "We're getting close. You need to turn up here." I said, "Okay." We got off the freeway and drove toward the docks. We drove up to the docks and parked. It was dark and quiet. There were a few dim lights on the docks and boats but it wasn't lit up much.

Kate started pointing and said, "Get that cart over there for our dive gear, so we won't have to carry it." I said, "Okay" and walked over to it. I pushed it back to the car. We unloaded our dive gear and put it on the cart. Kate said, "They have these carts so you can haul your stuff to and from the boats." I said, "Good, this is nice."

We pushed the cart to the boat and quietly started unloading it. We strapped our tanks against the inside of the boat next to the other tanks and put our dive gear next to the other dive gear. I pushed the cart over to where some other carts were. When I got back to the boat Kate pointed to some steps and quietly said, "Down there is where the bunks are. Come with me and I'll show you where the restroom is." I whispered, "Okay." We walked to the side of the boat then up toward the front to a small door on the side of the cabin. Kate started pointing at the door. I shook my head yes. Kate whispered, "Let's go downstairs, find our bunks and try to get some sleep." I whispered, "Okay, I'll follow you."

We walked back to the steps. Kate started quietly going down them. I stayed right behind her. There was a little night-light on so we could see a little, but not much. The bunks were on the walls of the boat and in the middle of the boat like bunk beds, uppers and lowers. Each had it's own curtain you could pull shut for privacy. I could hear someone snoring. Kate started pointing at me and at a top bunk. I thought this must be mine. I shook my head yes and climbed up into it. I shut my curtain and went to sleep.

The engines started and woke me up. I lifted my head up and could smell breakfast cooking. I was really tired so I put my head back down. I could feel the boat moving. After a little while I could hear the engines speed up. I kept on laying down then I fell back to sleep.

The engines slowed down and woke me up. I got out of my bunk and went upstairs. I saw Danny talking to a guy. Danny said, "Good morning." I said, "Good morning." Danny said, "Lee meet John." I said, "Hello John." John said, "Hello Lee." Danny and John started putting their dive gear together. I looked around and saw Kate sitting at a table in the galley. I waved at her. She waved back. Kate walked out from the galley and said, "I can't go on the first dive. My burst disk on my tank ruptured some way. I'm going to ask around but I've either got to find someone that has an extra burst disk or try to borrow a tank." Danny said, "See what you can do and if you can't figure out something. I'll see what I can do when we get back."

I said to Danny, "Since Kate can't go on this dive. Can I go diving with you?" Danny said, "Sure." I said, "Thanks" and hurried up and put my dive gear together. Danny and John started putting their wetsuits on. I started putting mine on. We put our dive gear on.

We were ready. Danny said, "Lee I know you've got a few dives but John is still a little new. So let's take it kind of easy." I said, "No Problem. I'll just stay nearby and try to stay out of the way." Danny said, "If you guys are ready let's get in and go down the anchor line." John and I said, "Okay."

We walked to the opening on the side of the boat where a little door was open. Danny said, "Lee why don't you go first and we'll meet at the anchor line." I said, "Okay." I put my fins on, my mask on, put my regulator in my mouth and aired up my BC. I stepped overboard. I splashed in the water and stayed still until I floated up to the surface. I took my regulator out of my mouth and started kicking up to the front of the boat. John came in and Danny right after him.

We were all three at the anchor line. Danny said, "I'll go first." I said, "I'll go last." John said jokingly, "That puts me in the middle then!" Danny got ready then started letting the air out of his BC and started going down. John got ready then started letting the air out of his BC and started going down. I got ready, reached over and grabbed the anchor line, started letting the air out of my BC and started going down. I looked down the anchor line then started looking around. The visibility was perfect. It seemed like I could see forever.

Danny was close to the bottom and John wasn't far from him. I kept going hand over hand down the anchor line. Danny and John just got to the bottom and started kicking away. I didn't have much further to go down so I let go of the anchor line and started kicking toward them. There were big rocks all over and some patches of tall kelp. Danny started going along looking at the bottom. John was following him and I wasn't too far behind them. We were going along the bottom and looking around.

I looked over and saw a big weird looking starfish and went over to it. I couldn't believe it. It was real big and had a bunch of legs. It didn't look like the normal starfish. I got close to it and examined it more closely. I thought man! This thing is weird looking.

I hurried up and caught back up with Danny and John. We kept going along looking around. John started having some kind of problem. Danny went over to him and started helping him. I stayed out of their way. Danny gave me the okay signal and started going again. John was right behind him. We kept going looking around. I thought what ever happened to John, Danny must have taken care of because John seems to be doing okay.

After awhile Danny looked at me and started pointing to the left. I looked in that direction. It was the anchor line. I gave him the okay signal. We kicked over to the anchor. Danny started up. John was staying right behind him. I started up behind John. We were all going slowly hand over hand up the anchor line. Danny stopped. John and I went up next to him. Danny gave us the stop hand signal and pointed to his dive watch. We were at fifteen feet. I thought oh he's stopping for our safety stop. I forgot about the safety stop. We waited and looked around at the bottom of the boat and down at the bottom. Danny started pointing up to us then he started going up. John followed him. I followed John.

We were on the surface. Danny said, "That was fun. It's so nice up here." I said, "It is. It's really good visibility and a lot of stuff to see here. What kind of starfish are those with a lot of legs?" Danny said, "Those are sunstars." I said, "I've never seen those before." Danny said, "They're big aren't they?" I said, "Yeah they are."

We kicked to the back of the boat and got on a big metal tailgate thing they let down for us. We took our fins off and walked up some steps to the deck. We took our dive gear off. Danny walked over to one of the showers that was mounted on the outside wall and started rinsing off. He said to me, "There's another one on that side." He was pointing to one not far from me. I said, "Okay, thanks." I went over to it and rinsed off. I walked back to my dive gear, took my wetsuit off, got out my towel and dried off.

I could see Kate sitting in the galley. I walked in. She was eating. Kate said, "You hungry? The cook is making hamburgers. Just let him know if you want one." She pointed at the cook. The cook said, "Would you like one?" I said, "Sure, I'm hungry." The cook said, "With fries?" I said, "Sure." I sat down next to Kate.

Kate said, "I got a new burst disk and my tank is aired up so I'll be ready at the next dive location." I said, "Good." The cook had my hamburger and fries ready. I went over, picked it up, grabbed a soda, sat back down and started eating. Other divers were starting to come into the galley and order their food.

The engines started. Then I could hear them pulling up the anchor. We were on our way to the next dive location. I said, "It sure is nice with the boat not being very crowded." Kate said, "Yeah there's plenty of room and no rushing. Just take it easy, do plenty of diving and eat all you want." I said, "I know this is nice." We finished eating and started talking to the other divers.

The captain started slowing the engines down and the deck hand dropped the anchor. Kate said, "Let's get ready." I said, "Okay." Kate and I walked to the back of the boat and started putting our wetsuits on. Kate said, "I'm taking my camera so let me know if you see anything good." I said, "Okay." Kate said, "I'm taking my dive light too so I can see under the rocks and in dark areas." I said, "That's a good idea. I will too." Danny said, "You'll get some good pictures out here" then he looked at me and said, "A good dive buddy will help their buddy take pictures like a team. Like steadying them and holding them in place while they're getting them." I said, "Okay. I can do that."

Kate and I put on our dive gear. I asked, "You ready?" Kate said, "Yeah, follow me." She started walking toward the front of the boat. I followed her. She unlatched and opened a little door just a little way from the front of the boat.

Kate said, "Have you ever gone in at the bow before?" I said, "No" and looked down. I thought man is it a long way down to the water. Kate said, "I like the bow better. You just jump in and you're at the anchor line." I said, "That is better."

Kate said, "Ready." I said, "Ready." We put our fins on, our mask on, aired up our BC's and put our regulators in our mouths. Kate stepped overboard. I walked up the edge and looked down. I was getting nervous and thought it was a long way down. I stepped overboard, it must have only been a couple of feet higher but I didn't think I was ever going to hit the water. Finally I landed in the water. I floated back up. We kicked to the anchor line. Kate said, "Ready?" I said, "Ready. I'll follow you."

We let the air out of our BC's and started going down the anchor line, hand over hand. I was looking around then up at the boat. I thought this is so nice to be in such clear water. This is really neat. I kept looking around as we were going down.

We were on the bottom. We were surging a little bit back and forth. Kate started taking pictures. I helped her whenever I could. I would steady her in the surge and hold her in place while she took pictures. She kept taking pictures of anything that moved, fish, animal or plant.

We were going along the bottom, stopping and taking pictures then going a little further. Kate signaled to me that she was out of film. I gave her the okay signal. We kept going and looking around.

Kate started pointing at her computer then pointing back. I checked my air. I was down to sixteen hundred pounds. I gave her the okay signal. We turned around and started back toward the boat.

We kept going slow and looking around. I could see the anchor line. I waved at Kate and pointed at it. Kate gave me the okay signal. We kicked over to it and started up it. We were slowly going up and kept looking around.

We were on the surface. We took our regulators out of our mouths, kicked to the back of the boat and got on the metal tailgate. We took off our mask. The deckhand quickly walked down the steps and over to Kate. He took off her fins for her and grabbed her mask. He carried them up and put them up on the deck. He came back down, reached for my fins and mask. I handed them to him. He carried them up and put them on the deck. Then he came back down and started helping Kate up the steps. I was following them.

We took our dive gear off, walked to the showers and rinsed off. We walked back to our dive gear, took our wetsuits off and dried off. We packed all of our dive gear and put it up. The deckhand walked over to Kate and said, "You want a dry wetsuit in the morning?" Kate said, "Sure." The deck hand said, "Let me have it. I'll hang it in the engine compartment and it'll dry there." Kate grabbed her wetsuit and handed it to him. She started walking with him. He opened a small door and went down into the engine compartment. He came back up and said, "I'll get it for you in the morning." Kate said, "Okay."

We could smell something cooking. Kate said, "I'm hungry." I said, "Me too." We walked into the galley. Several people were sitting around eating and talking. Kate asked the cook, "What's for dinner?" The cook said, "Lobster or hamburgers." Kate said, "I'll take lobster." The cook looked at me. I said, "I'll take a hamburger." The cook said, "Give me a few minutes."

The captain started the engines. We heard the anchor being pulled up. We were on our way. The cook waved at Kate then at me. We walked over, got our food, sat back down and started eating. One of the other divers started telling jokes. We were all listening and laughing.

Everyone was sitting around and talking. It was late and dark. Danny said, "I'm going to call it a day." Everyone said good night. Danny got up and walked away. I said to Kate, "Danny sure is funny. He seems like a good guy and a real good dive instructor but he just does some strange stuff sometimes. You never really know what he's going to do next. I like him though and I like diving with him." Kate said, "He is a little different sometimes but he's one of the best instructors and he's been diving a long time. You can always count on him too." I said, "I thought he seemed to know what he was doing when he was diving."

A little later I said, "I'm a little tired. I think I'll call it a day too." Everyone said goodnight to me. I walked downstairs, got in my bunk and fell asleep.

Monday morning …

The captain started the engines and it woke me up. I lifted my head up and could smell breakfast cooking again. I thought man it's already morning! I can sleep well on this boat for some reason. I didn't feel it rock or move at all during the night. I laid my head back down. I could feel the boat moving. I could hear the engines speed up. I rolled over and fell back to sleep

The captain slowed the engines down and that woke me up. I got out of my bunk and went upstairs. People were getting ready, putting their wetsuits and dive gear on. Kate was sitting in the galley. I walked over to Kate. She asked, "Are you about ready to go diving?" I said, "Yeah. I'm ready." Kate said, "Let's go."

We walked to the back of the boat. The deckhand started waving at Kate then walked to the engine compartment and went down. He came back up with her wetsuit, walked over to her and handed it to her. Kate said, "Oooooh! It's warm, nice and dry." We both started putting our wetsuits on. I said, "Oooooh! Mine is cold and wet!"

Danny was only a few feet from Kate and I. He had his wetsuit on and was bending over just about to grab his dive gear. All of a sudden he started saying, "Oooooh, oooooh, oooooh" and stood straight up, put his hands and arms straight out from his sides and lifted his left leg out sideways. He was standing on one leg. He stood still and looked at us and said with a relief, "Ahhhhh, now my wetsuit is warm." Kate said, "Oh you're gross" and started moving away from him. I started laughing really hard and watching them.

Kate looked over at me and said, "I'm taking my camera again so let me know if you see anything." I said, "Okay." Kate and I put our dive gear on and walked up to the front of the boat. Kate unlatched and opened the little door. Kate said, "You ready?" I said, "Yeah. I'll follow you." We put our fins on, our mask on, aired up our BC's and put our regulators in our mouths. Kate stepped overboard. She floated up and moved out of the way. I stepped overboard and floated up. We kicked over to the anchor line.

I said, "I'll follow you and help you when I can." Kate said, "Okay." We started letting the air out of our BC's and started going down the anchor line, hand over hand. I started looking down at the bottom, at the anchor line and all around. We kept going down.

We were on the bottom. We started slowly going along. Kate started taking pictures. I saw a lobster under some kelp. I went over to it and pointed at it. Kate took some pictures of it. It was nice here, no surge at all. I saw a clam stuck onto a big rock. Kate took pictures of it. She started pointing at something and started taking pictures of it. It was a fancy looking little blue slug like thing. Kate signaled to me that she was already out of film. I gave her the okay signal.

We kept going and looking around. We were looking in the cracks of the rocks and under them. I was down to fifteen hundred pounds of air. I signaled to Kate for us to start back toward the boat. Kate gave me the okay signal. We turned around and started back. On the way back we could see the boat floating on the surface. We could see the anchor line going down to the bottom. I thought this is so nice with the water being so clear. We kicked over to the anchor and started up. We were going slow, looking around on the way up.

We were about five feet from the surface. Kate was trying to dump the air out of her BC while she was holding her camera and dive light. She was having trouble holding onto everything. She accidentally dropped her dive light. It was falling toward the bottom. I turned around and started down as fast as I could go chasing after it. It was just a little bit out of my reach. I kept trying to catch it. It landed on the bottom. I went down, picked it up and then started back up. I could see Kate on the surface looking down at me. I went up next to her, aired up my BC, took my regulator out of my mouth and my mask off. I said, "You dropped your dive light. I went and got it. I tried to catch it but I couldn't so I had to go all the way to the bottom." Kate said, "Thanks, I didn't even know I dropped it." I said, "I didn't think you did. You were having trouble letting air out of your BC when you dropped it." Kate said, "Yeah. I was having a little trouble. We got some good pictures though. I'll get you a set of all the pictures when I get them developed." I said, "Okay, thanks." Kate said, "I've already used all the cameras I brought. I didn't think I would use them that fast." I said, "You did take a lot of pictures. I hope they all turn out. Man something smells good." Kate said, "I think its brownies." I said, "I hope you're right."

We kicked over to the back of the boat and got on the metal tailgate. The deck hand quickly walked down the steps and took Kate's fins off her feet. He then came over and took off mine. He carried them up and put them on the deck. He came back down the steps and got our mask and Kate's camera. He went up and put them next to our fins. He came back down and started helping Kate up the steps. I walked up the steps behind them.

We started taking our dive gear off. Danny and John walked up from their dive and started taking off their dive gear. Kate walked over to one of the showers and started rinsing off. I walked over to the other one. Danny started taking his wetsuit off and sniffing with his nose at his wetsuit. He said, "Boy that stinks" and looked at me. I started laughing so hard I could barely stand up.

We finished rinsing off and walked back to our dive gear. We took our wetsuits off and dried off. I said, "Let's go eat." Kate said, "Okay." We walked to the galley. The cook had sandwiches sitting on one of the tables and brownies sitting on one of the other tables. I said to the cook, "They smell so good." The cook said, "Thank you." Kate and I both got a plate and walked over and grabbed a sandwich, chips, brownies and sodas. We sat down and started eating. People were coming back from diving, coming in, getting sandwiches and sitting down. Everyone was eating and talking.

The engines started and we could hear them pulling up the anchor. We were on our way to the next dive location. We all kept sitting around talking. After awhile Danny said, "We're going to stay at the next dive location until after dark so you can do a day and night dive there if you want." I asked Kate if she wanted to do a night dive. Kate said, "Sure." Danny said, "It's going to take us a while to get there."

A while later the captain slowed down the boat and pulled up close to one of the islands. The deckhand dropped the anchor. We all started walking to the back of the boat. Kate and I started putting on our wetsuits. Kate said, "Do you want to go toward the deeper water on the day dive and the shallower water on the night dive?" I said, "Sounds good to me."

We finished putting our wetsuits on and put our dive gear on. We walked up to the front of the boat. Kate unlatched and opened the little door. I said, "They must shut the door when they move around." Kate said, "Yeah they do. You ready?" I said, "I'll follow you." We put our fins on, our mask on, aired up our BC's and put our regulators in our mouths. Kate stepped overboard, floated up and moved out of the way. I stepped overboard and floated up. We kicked over to the anchor line. We let the air out of our BC's and started going down the anchor line. I started looking around and down at the bottom as we were slowly going down.

We were on the bottom. We started going out away from the island. It was gradually getting a little deeper. It was a sandy bottom with some kelp and rocks but there wasn't much to look at. We kept going and looking around.

I could see a small rope up ahead of us that looked like a small anchor line. I waved at Kate and pointed to it. It went from the bottom up to the surface but there wasn't a boat up there. We started toward it. It was tied to a lobster cage. We started getting close to it.

Something was in it. We went up to it and started looking at it. It was a three foot horn shark all crammed into it. It must have swam into it and got stuck. Kate and I looked at each other then looked back at it.

It was alive but not moving much. Kate stuck her hand into the opening where the lobsters are suppose to go in at and grabbed the sharks tail. The shark didn't move. It must have been in the cage a long time. Kate looked at me like what are we going to do. We both started looking around at the cage really close.

It was a wire cage with a maze of wires made into compartments. A lobster would find it easy to get in but then would become trapped. It would be hard for us to get the shark out unless we opened the lid, which had a plastic seal on it that would need to be broken. Who ever owned the trap must have put the seal on it so they could tell if divers were taking their lobsters. I stuck my hand into the opening and grabbed the sharks tail and started pulling on it trying to guide it backwards. Kate started poking and pushing on its sides when it would get stuck.

It started moving and trying to get loose from us by going forward, further into the cage but it didn't have much energy. I kept pulling it backward trying not to hurt it. Kate kept poking and pushing it on its sides. It would get stuck and we would get it free over and over. It was getting close to being out of the cage.

We got it out. I was holding it in my hands, pointing it away from us. It was bending back and forth like it was trying to bite us. Kate jumped back out of the way. I held onto it, pointed it away from us and let go of it. It slowly swam off about twenty feet away from us, went down to the bottom and stopped. We stayed where we were and watched it. After a little while it started swimming off.

I was down to twelve hundred pounds of air. I pointed at my pressure gauge and back toward the boat. Kate gave me the okay signal. We turned around and started back. We could see the boat. We went over to the anchor line and started up it. We were slowly going up.

We were on the surface. We aired up our BC's, took our regulators out of our mouths and our mask off. I said, "We did our good deed for the day." Kate said, "We did. It was sad seeing it stuck in there." I said, "It would have been easy to just open it up if it didn't have the seal." Kate said, "Yeah but they would have thought we stole their lobsters. I'm glad we got it out without breaking the seal."

I said, "Me too." I started sniffing and said, "Man something smells good." Kate said, "It smells like steaks." I said, "I bet you're right."

We kicked over to the back of the boat, got on the metal tailgate and took our fins off. The deck hand quickly walked down the steps, got Kate's fins and mask then reached over and got mine. He carried them up and put them on the deck. We started getting out. The deckhand came back down the steps and started helping Kate. I walked up the steps behind them.

We took our dive gear off. Kate walked over to one shower and I walked over to the other one. We rinsed off. We walked back to our dive gear, took our wetsuits off and dried off.

We walked into the galley. There was some pies sitting on the tables. Kate and I walked up to the cook. He was cooking away. Kate asked, "What smells so good, steaks?" The cook said, "Yes. You ready for one?" Kate said, "Yes, they smell so good." The cook looked at me. I said, "I'll take one too."

The cook gave us each a plate with a steak, mashed potatoes, green beans and a roll on them. We sat down and started eating. The other divers started coming back in from their dives. They were coming in, getting their food, sitting down and eating it. Everyone was eating and talking.

The sun was starting to go down. We finished eating then we got a piece of pie. Kate asked, "Are you about ready to do a night dive?" I said, "I'm ready as soon as I eat my pie." Kate said, "Me too." We finished eating our pie then we walked to the back of the boat and started putting our wetsuits on. John walked up and said, "You guys going to do the night dive?" Kate said, "Yes." John asked, "Do you mind if I go with you?" Kate said, "Not at all."

John quickly walked back to his dive gear and put his wetsuit on. He carried his dive gear over, close to us. We all cracked open a chemstick and tied them to our tanks. We put our dive gear on and walked up to the front of the boat.

We looked out in the water between the boat and the island. We could see the divers chemsticks glowing and dive lights looking around underwater. We turned on our dive lights. John said, "I'm still pretty new so I'll just follow you guys if that's okay." Kate said, "That's okay. We're going to stay in the shallow water anyway. You guys ready?" I said, "I am" then I looked over at John and said, "Have you ever gone in at the bow before?" John said, "No this is the first time." I said, "It's just as easy just a little further to the water but you're already at the anchor line." John said, "Good."

We put our fins on, our mask on, aired up our BC's and put our regulators in our mouths. Kate stepped overboard, floated up and moved out of the way. I said, "Go ahead John." John stepped overboard, floated up and moved out of the way. I stepped overboard. We kicked over to the anchor line. Kate said, "You guys ready?" John and I said, "Yes."

Kate started letting the air out of her BC and started going down the anchor line. I let the air out of my BC and started down. I looked back up and saw John up a little way from me. He seemed to be doing okay. I started looking around. The water was really dark. We kept slowly going down.

We were on the bottom. We all gave each other the okay signal. Kate started going toward the island and other divers. I started following her and John was right behind me. There were rocks all over. We started looking around, under the rocks and in between them with our dive lights. It seemed like there were lobsters everywhere in the rocks. Some of the openings had two or three of them together, like a family. As I would get close to some of them they would come out like they wanted to greet me, then they would walk backwards back into their hiding place.

We kept looking around. I looked under one rock that had an opening under it like a little cave. There was a big lobster in it. I shined my dive light right on him then stuck my hand under the rock and tried to grab him. He started going backwards away from me. I quickly grabbed his antenna like ear things and started pulling him. He started fighting and moving around really hard. His antenna broke off. He took off backward and got away. I had his antenna in my hand. I thought oh great why did I do that? I could have kicked myself for that. I felt bad now.

We kept looking around and under the rocks. I didn't try to catch anymore lobsters. I just looked at them. John came over next to me and started pointing at his pressure gauge. He must be low on air. I shined my dive light over in front of Kate. She looked over at us. I shined my dive light on my pressure gauge and pointed back toward the boat. Kate gave me the okay signal.

We started toward the boat. We could see the lights from the boat and started toward them. We were looking for the anchor line. Kate saw it and started shining her dive light on it. She started going toward it.

We went over to the anchor and started up. We were slowly going up, looking around on our way. I thought man, its more lit up now! They must have turned on some more lights.

We were on the surface. We aired up our BC's, took our regulators out of our mouths and our mask off. John said, "There are a lot of lobsters here." I said, "I've never seen so many." Kate said, "Yeah this is a good place for lobster." I looked up at the boat. There were lights on all around it.

We kicked over to the back of the boat, got on the metal tailgate and took our fins off. We helped each other get out of the water and onto the back of the boat. We started up the steps. John said, "Thanks for letting me go with you guys." Kate and I said, "You're welcome."

We took our dive gear off, walked over to the showers and rinsed off. We walked back to our dive gear, took our wetsuits off and dried off. The deckhand walked back from the front of the boat. He walked over, picked up Kate's wetsuit and gave her the thumbs up signal. Kate said, "Thank you." We packed our dive gear and put it up. We walked into the galley, got some more pie, a soda, sat down and started eating.

The other divers started coming back in from their dives. They were coming in, getting a piece of pie and sodas too. We were all eating and talking. The captain started the engines then we heard them pulling up the anchor. We were on our way.

A little while later Kate said, "Let's go on the top deck and look at the stars." She stood up and started walking outside. We walked out with her. We climbed up a ladder to the next deck. There were bench-like seats on both sides behind the wheelhouse, where we could see the captain driving the boat. We all started looking at the dark sky and bright stars. Stars were everywhere. It was a nice clear and warm night.

A while later Danny said, "I think I'm calling it a day." We all said, "Okay we'll see you tomorrow." Danny said, "Okay" then started down the ladder. I said, "I think I will too. I'm a little worn out." Everyone said, "Okay we'll see you tomorrow." I climbed down the ladder, walked down to the bunks and climbed into my bunk. I fell to sleep.

I woke up. I needed to go to the restroom. It was quiet, the engines weren't running and nothing was making any noise. I quietly got out of my bunk and walked upstairs. It was very quiet and really dark. There was a little bit of light downstairs but you couldn't see much at all up on the deck. I walked to the restroom.

I came out of the restroom and looked out from the side of the boat. It looked strange and black, no stars, no light at all, nothing - just solid black. I looked almost straight up and could see stars. I thought man that's a cliff right next to the boat. I started looking around. We were in a cove with cliffs all around us. It looked like we barely fit in it. I thought no wonder the boat doesn't rock at night. It was an eerie feeling. I went back downstairs and got in my bunk and fell back to sleep.

Tuesday ...

The captain started the engines and woke me up. I lifted my head up and smelled the good food cooking. I couldn't believe it was morning already. I laid my head back down. I heard the engines speed up. I rolled over and fell back to sleep.

The captain slowed the engines down and it woke me up again. I got out of my bunk and went upstairs. People were getting ready putting their wetsuits and dive gear on. I walked into the galley. Kate was eating breakfast. Kate asked, "You hungry? The cook will fix you breakfast or there's donuts." I said, "A donut sounds good and some coffee." I walked over, got a donut, a cup of coffee, sat down next to Kate and started eating.

The deckhand dropped the anchor and the captain shut off the engines. Kate said, "You missed it. I drove the boat last night." I said, "You did?" Kate said, "Yeah I went in, talked to the captain and he let me drive it for awhile." I said, "I bet that was fun. I've never driven a boat this big." Kate said, "I haven't either."

We finished eating and drinking our coffee. Kate asked, "You ready?" I said, "Yeah I'm ready if you are." Kate said, "Let's go." We walked to the back of the boat. The deckhand looked at us, walked over to the engine compartment, went down, got Kate's wetsuit then back up and handed her dry wetsuit to her. Kate said, "Thank you" and put it next to her dive gear. Kate and I started putting our dive gear together.

Kate said to me, "This is my hundredth dive." A guy close to us looked over at her and said real loud, "Hey everyone this is Kate's hundredth dive. We need to celebrate." A few divers started saying, "Hip hip hurray." A couple of other divers walked up to her and said, "Congratulations." I said, "Wow! You've got a hundred dives. This will only be my forty forth." Kate said, "You're kidding. You've already got forty-four dives. You have been diving a lot. It seems like it's taken me forever to get a hundred dives and you've already got forty four." I said, "David and Deb have been keeping me busy." Kate said, "I guess they have."

Kate and I started putting our wetsuits on. I said "Eew ... a wet wetsuit sure is wet and cold in the morning." Kate said, "I know what you mean" as she was putting her warm, dry wetsuit on.

We finished putting our wetsuits on then started putting on our dive gear. Kate said, "Let's do a safety stop coming back on this dive. We haven't been doing them." I said, "You're right. I forgot all about the safety stops."

We finished putting our dive gear on and walked up to the front of the boat. Kate unlatched and opened the little door. Kate said, "I'm ready." I said, "I'll be right behind you." We put our fins on, our mask on, aired up our BC's and put our regulators in our mouths. Kate stepped overboard, floated up and moved out of the way. I stepped overboard. We kicked over to the anchor line.

We let the air out of our BC's and started going down the anchor line. I started looking around staying right behind Kate. We kept slowly going down.

We were on the bottom. There were big rocks and kelp all around. We started going slow looking around, going over and around the big rocks and kelp. Kate started waving at me and pointing ahead of us toward one of the rocks. It was a baby hornshark about a foot long. Kate went over to it and picked it up with her left hand. It was bending side to side like it was trying to get away from her. I went up next to her. We were both looking at it.

Kate stuck her right hand pointing finger up to its head like she was going to pet it. It snapped and bit the end part of her glove on her finger. It was holding it in its mouth. Kate was all shocked and surprised. I was too. It was so small and harmless looking to bite like that. Kate looked at me while the end of her glove was in the shark's mouth. I could tell she was laughing. I was thinking how glad I was that it only bit her glove and not her finger.

Kate started trying to get her glove out of the shark's mouth. She started pulling on her glove, squeezing the little shark's jaws in from the sides and pulling up and down. Finally she got it loose. She put the little shark back down on the rock.

We started going again while looking around. I heard a noise. It was a weird sounding noise. I heard it again and again. It was spear guns. I thought oh man I wonder where they are and where they're shooting. I couldn't tell which direction the sound was coming from but it sounded close. Kate looked at me. I made my arms like I was holding a gun. Kate gave me the okay signal. We stayed still and started looking all around us then I saw a couple of guys not far from us going through the kelp. I signaled to Kate for us to go in the opposite direction from them. She gave me the okay signal. We both started kicking fast and getting away from them.

We slowed down and kept going. We didn't hear anymore spear guns. Kate pointed at her pressure gauge. I gave her the okay signal. We turned around and started back toward the boat. We were looking around, going slow and looking for the boat or the anchor line. Kate started pointing. It was the anchor line. We kicked over to it and started going up.

We were slowly going up. Looking around on our way up. I started looking at the bottom of the boat. Something was next to it. It looks like a small boat. I grabbed Kate's fin. She looked down at me. I pointed at the small boat. She looked up and started looking at it too. We kept looking at it as we were getting closer to the surface.

Kate started waving at me to stop then started pointing to her computer. I thought oh man! I almost forgot the safety stop again! We were at fifteen feet. We kept looking around and over at the small boat. We could see two other divers that were about fifty feet from the back of our boat, on the surface kicking toward the boat. It looked like the little boat was about eighteen feet long. It was tied to the side of our boat. It looked a little weird looking up and seeing two boats tied together. I thought it must be a visitor. Maybe someone the captain knows or someone else on the boat knew them.

Kate started pointing up. I gave her the okay signal. We started up. We were on the surface next to the anchor line. We aired up our BC's, took our regulators out of our mouths and our mask off. I said, "I can't believe that little shark almost bit your finger." Kate said, "I can't either. It had my glove and wouldn't let go." I said, "That was funny. You should have seen the look on your face when it bit your glove." Kate said, "It scared me. I didn't expect it to bite me!"

I said, "Man, I like coming up and smelling that good cooking." Kate said, "I know it's so nice to just climb onto the boat coming back and just step off to go in too. This is my favorite way of diving." I said, "Mine too. I really like it." Kate said, "It's so easy and no sand to walk on or get in your dive gear." I said, "I know it is nice."

We kicked over close to the back of the boat. Those two other divers were on the metal tailgate. They were taking their fins off and getting ready to get out. I looked up on the deck. There was a guy in what looked like a cop uniform standing at the top of the steps looking down at them. He looked over at Kate and I too. We stayed still, floated in the water and watched. The divers started walking up the steps. The guy that looked like a cop got in front of them at the top of the steps and stopped them. He said something to the first diver. The diver opened his bag up. It looked like it had a fish or lobster in it. The uniformed guy started looking in the diver's bag. I said, "What's going on?" Kate said, "Fish and Game. I'll tell you later." I said, "Okay." He started looking in the other diver's bag. Kate asked, "You ready to get out?" I said, "Yeah I guess but he makes me a little nervous." Kate said, "He won't bother us."

We got on the metal tailgate and took our fins off. We started getting out. The Fish and Game Officer kept watching us. Kate started walking up the steps. I was right behind her.

Kate got to the top of the steps. The Fish and Game Officer got in front of her and said, "Were you doing any fishing?" Kate said, "No just diving." He said,

"Thank you" and moved over to the side. Kate walked past him. As I walked up he stayed over at the side. I said, "I'm with her, just diving, no fishing." He said, "Thank you."

We walked over close to the showers and took our dive gear off. We started rinsing off in the showers. I kept glancing over at the Fish and Game Officer and watching him as he was checking everyone as they came onto the boat. He would just look into their bag then they would go on past him.

We walked back to our dive gear, took our wetsuits off and dried off. We walked into the galley, got a soda and sat down. Kate said, "Fish and Game checks everyone's bags for illegal fish and lobster. If anyone has something that is illegal they get a ticket and the captain of the boat gets a ticket." I said, "That doesn't seem fair." Kate said, "I know it isn't. What they do is sit off in the distance where you don't notice them. Then they watch the dive boats with binoculars. When the divers go down they hurry up, go get on the dive boat and check everyone's bags as they come up." I said, "Man that sure is sneaky." Kate said, "I know."

Kate and I walked up to the cook. He was cooking away. Kate said, "Whatcha cooking?" The cook said, "Meatloaf and hamburgers which one would you like?" Kate said, "Meatloaf." I said, "Me too." I breathed in real deep it smelled so good. The cook gave us our plates. It had meatloaf, mashed potatoes with gravy, peas and rolls on them. We sat back down and started eating. The other divers were coming in, getting their food, sitting down and eating it too.

We heard the Fish and Game Officer start his boat. We could hear him leaving. After a little while the captain started the engines and the deckhand pulled up the anchor.

We were on our way to the next dive location. We finished eating then sat around talking. Danny was on the other side of the boat. He started walking around and talking to the divers. He walked over close to us and said, "This will be our last dive." A diver next to Kate said, "Already? I don't want to go back. I've got to go back to work." Kate said, "Yeah! Let's stay another day." I said, "Yeah or two!" Kate asked Danny, "Did Fish and Game get anyone?" Danny said, "No we didn't have any trouble." Kate said, "Good."

After awhile the captain started slowing the boat down. The deckhand dropped the anchor and the captain turned off the engines. We all started walking to the back of the boat.

Kate and I put our wetsuits on and started putting our dive gear on. Kate said, "I can't believe this is our last dive already?" I said, "I can't either. This has been so much fun." We finished putting our dive gear on and walked up to the front of the boat. I unlatched and opened the little door.

Kate asked, "You ready?" I said, "Yeah if you are" then I looked down over the side of the boat and said, "What's that on the bottom? It looks like a lot of different colored trash." Kate started looking down at the bottom too. The water was crystal clear and you could see the bottom really good. Kate said, "I think those are brittle stars." I said, "Brittle stars! What are those?" Kate said, "They're little starfish with long legs. Let's go check them out." I said, "Okay."

We put our fins on, our mask on, aired up our BC's and put our regulators in our mouths. Kate stepped overboard and moved out of the way. I stepped overboard. We kicked over to the anchor line.

We let the air out of our BC's and started going down the anchor line. I kept looking down at the bottom as we were going down, there were so many different colors down there. We kept slowly going down.

We were getting close to bottom. We were thirty-five feet deep. Kate was right. They were little different colored starfish looking things with long skinny legs and they were everywhere. They were so thick that they covered the whole bottom! I tried not to touch the bottom or I would have smashed them. I picked up one and started looking at it then picked up a hand full of them. They were moving their little legs all around. I looked at them then put them back down.

We started going along the bottom looking at them and trying not to smash them. We saw three divers up ahead of us. Kate started pointing at them and giving me the okay signal. I gave her the okay signal back. We started hurrying trying to catch up with them. We got close to them. They looked back and started waving at us. We waved back. We all stayed close together and kept going while looking around.

I checked my air. I was down to fifteen hundred pounds. I waved at Kate and pointed back toward the boat. Kate gave me the okay signal. We turned around and started back. We could see the boat on the surface. It looked like it was a long way away from us. We kept going toward it. We could see the anchor line. We kicked over to it and started going up.

We were slowly going up. I kept looking down at the brittle stars as I was going up. I noticed Kate closely watching her computer then she stopped. We were at fifteen feet. We stopped and started looking around at the boat and down at the brittle stars. After a few minutes Kate started pointing up. I gave her the okay signal. We started up.

We were on the surface. We aired up our BC's, took our regulators out of our mouths and our mask off. I said, "I can't believe all those brittle stars down there.

They're so thick." Kate said, "I know there's a bunch of them. I've never seen this many."

We kicked over to the back of the boat, got on the metal tailgate and took our fins off. The deck hand quickly walked down the steps. He got Kate's fins and mask. Then he reached over and grabbed mine. He carried them up and put them on the deck. We started getting out. The deckhand came back down the steps and started helping Kate up the steps. I walked up the steps behind them.

We took our dive gear off, walked over to the showers and rinsed off. We walked back to our dive gear, took our wetsuits off and dried off. We packed all our dive gear and put it up.

We walked into the galley. There were chocolate cakes sitting on the tables. I said, "Man those look good." Kate said, "They do." We walked up to the cook. Kate said, "What smells so good?" The cook said, "Chicken and hamburgers." Kate said, "I'll have chicken." I said, "So will I." The cook gave us each a plate with chicken, fries, corn and a roll.

We sat down and started eating. The other divers were coming in, getting their food, sitting down and eating it. We all started talking. Kate and I finished eating then got some chocolate cake and started eating it.

The captain started the engines and the deckhand pulled up the anchor. We were on our way back home. We finished eating our cake and sat around talking to everyone. A while later Kate said, "I'm going to go pack all my clothes and stuff." I said, "I had better do that too. I'll go with you." We walked downstairs and packed everything. I said, "That cake sure was good. I think I could use another piece." Kate said, "Me too."

We walked back up the galley. The cook was cleaning everything up and all the tables were clean. Kate said to the cook, "Is there anymore cake?" The cook said, "There sure is." He walked over behind the counter and handed us both a paper plate with a slice of cake on it. We both said, "Thanks." We walked over, got a soda, sat down and started eating.

We finished eating and sat around talking to everyone. The captain started slowing down the engines. He pulled the boat into the marina and up to the dock. The deckhand jumped off the boat and tied it up.

We heard some yelling and looked over at a guy yelling on one of the other boats. He was mad. I asked Kate, "I wonder what's going on?" Kate said, "I don't know but he sure is mad."

We went downstairs and got our stuff then came back up. Kate was looking around then said, "There's a empty cart over there. I'll go get it." I said, "Okay." She got off the boat, walked over, got it and pushed it back. We unloaded all of our dive gear off the boat onto the cart. The captain and deckhand were standing on the dock. The captain said, "Thanks for coming. I hope you had fun." I said, "Man that was a lot of fun." Kate said, "Thanks for letting me drive the boat." The captain said, "You're welcome."

I started pushing the cart down the dock then toward the car. Kate said, "I'll be right back" and walked over to one of the guys that was on our boat. She started talking to him. I kept pushing the cart toward the car. Kate walked back and said, "You know that guy that was mad? Fish and Game gave him a ticket." I said, "That must be some ticket." Kate said, "I think it is."

I pushed the cart up to the car. We loaded all our dive gear in the car. Kate pushed the cart over close to some other carts.

We were on our way back home. The sun was going down. I said, "That sure was fun. I can't believe how all those dives were so much different from each other." Kate said, "I know it's fun diving there."

We pulled into the driveway and parked. We started unloading our dive gear. I helped Kate carry hers to her car. Kate said, "Thanks for doing the driving." I said, "You're welcome." Kate said, "I'm going home and resting." I said, "That's what I'm going to do too." Kate got in her car and drove off. I rinsed all my dive gear off and put it up.

Wednesday …

I loaded my tank in the car, drove to the dive shop, carried it in and put it at the filling area. I walked to the front of the dive shop. Ron was behind the counter working on some paperwork. Ron said, "Hello. How was the three day Channel Island dive trip?" I said, "It was great. I didn't get seasick, I ate all the time, I slept good, we did a lot of diving and the visibility was perfect on every dive." Ron said, "Good I'm glad you had a good time." I said, "Can I get some air. I only have one tank that needs filled this time. The one I took on the trip and I would also like to look at the cameras. I like the one Kate has." Ron said, "Those really aren't cameras. They're housings. You put a disposable camera inside the housing. It's waterproof so it keeps the camera dry."

We walked over to the small counter at the side of the dive shop. Ron opened up the showcase, got one out, opened it up and said, "See you put a camera in here." I said, "Oh that's pretty simple." Ron said, "You can buy the housings alone or as a kit that comes with the strobe and two lenses that you put in front of the housing. One is for macro pictures so you can get close ups and the other is a correcting lens, with it if you take a picture of someone it will focus on them and the background. Without it the background will be blurry. The strobe is the flash but since it's on this arm" he started pointing to a plastic bar "It holds the strobe about a foot away from the camera. So when you take the picture the flash will be from a different angle, that way you won't see the particles in the water. These housings work really well." I said, "I think I'll take the kit." Ron said, "You'll have fun with it." I paid for it then we walked back to the filling area.

Ron filled my tank. I said, "Thanks Ron." I carried my camera housing and tank out to the car. I started driving home.

As I was driving up the driveway I noticed a package on the porch. I parked, grabbed the camera housing, walked over, picked up the package and carried it in the house. I opened up the package. It was my new dive light and dive knife. I walked back out and unloaded my tank.

Thursday morning ...

I called Deb and said, "I bought a camera! Let's go diving at Shaw's and try it out." Deb said, "Okay but I can only do one." I said, "That's okay." Deb said, "Pick me up."

I loaded my dive gear in the car and drove over to Deb's house. Deb loaded her dive gear. We were on our way to Shaw's Cove. I said, "Man that was fun on the three day boat trip. They treat you like a king. We did a lot of diving, eating and I slept good. At night they pull the boat into coves, so you don't feel the boat move or rock at all. Diving is just a few steps and you're in the water. Getting out is a few steps up the back of the boat and you're on the deck. They even help you get out of the water and help you take your fins off especially if you're female. I had so much fun." Deb said, "I wish I would have gone." I said, "You have to try to go next time." Deb said, "I will."

We drove by next to the water where we could see the waves. Deb said, "Oh good they're small." I said, "Good." We drove up to Shaw's and parked. We got out and put our dive gear together. I put a disposable camera into the camera housing, attached the strobe and put the corrective lens on. We put our wetsuits and our dive gear on. I grabbed the camera.

We walked over to the steps, down to the beach and started walking across the sand. I said, "Don't forget your BC." We both aired them up. We got in the water, put our fins on and started kicking out. I said, "If you see anything good let me know and I'll take a picture of it." Deb said, "Okay I'll keep an eye out." I said, "I was looking at my book that has beach dives. It shows a rock arch just a little way out. Lets go down and look for it." Deb said, "Okay." We put our mask on, our regulators in our mouths and started letting the air out of our BC's.

We were on the bottom. We started slowly going and looking around. I saw a small starfish. I took a picture of it. I took Deb's picture then a picture of a big rock, a bunch of muscle shells and some more of Deb.

We kept slowly going. I was taking pictures of everything. Deb started pointing. It was the rock arch. I took some pictures of it. We looked at it for awhile then we started going out deeper. I kept looking for something good to take a picture of. Deb started looking into a hole on the reef. She started waving both her hands at me to come over and look into it. She started putting her fingers to her thumbs on both of her hands making her hands like they were eating. I quickly went over to see what she was looking at. She moved back and I looked into the hole. There was a bunch of small red shrimp. I gave her the okay signal and started taking pictures of them.

Deb put her head up close to mine and started looking into the hole with me. Deb grabbed my shoulder and started shaking her head no then started doing the same thing again with her hands like they were eating. She started looking into the hole again. She was staying still and staring into it. She kept looking into the hole then started quickly waving at me and pointing into it again. I quickly put my face up close to hers and looked into it again. It was an eel. It was opening and closing its mouth like Deb was doing her hands. I moved my head back away from it to see what it was going to do. It seemed like it wasn't going to try to bite us. I put my head over next to Deb's. We both started watching it. It kept doing its mouth just like Deb was doing with her hands. I thought they must do their mouths like that for some reason.

I held the camera up close to the hole and took pictures of it until I was out of film. We watched it for awhile then Deb started pointing out. I gave her the okay signal. We started slowly going and looking around. We were at thirty feet. I was down to thirteen hundred pounds of air. I signaled to Deb for us to turn around. She gave me the okay signal.

We turned around and started back in. We were going slow and looking around. I checked my air. I was down to four hundred pounds. We were at ten feet. I signaled to Deb for us to go up. She gave me the okay signal. We started going up.

We were on the surface. We aired up our BC's, took our regulators out of our mouths and our mask off. Deb said, "That eel was neat and did you see all those red shrimp." I said, "Yeah I wonder why they were so close to the eel. I thought it was going to try to bite us at first the way it was moving its mouth." Deb said, "I think that's natural for them to do that." I said, "That's weird." We floated on the surface and rested.

I asked, "You ready to get out?" Deb said, "Yeah I guess so." We kicked in close, took our fins off and got out. Deb said, "Here get my weights" and handed them to me. I grabbed her fins and mask. We walked across the beach and started up the steps. Deb stopped and rested like usual all the way up. We walked over to the car.

We took our dive gear and wetsuits off then loaded everything in the car. We were on our way to Deb's house. Deb said, "I probably won't be able to go diving again for a few days." I said, "Just let me know when you're ready." Deb said, "Okay."

We drove up to Deb's house. She unloaded her dive gear. I drove home, unloaded my dive gear, rinsed it off and put it up.

Friday morning ...

I loaded the two empty tanks in the car, drove to the dive shop, carried them in and put them at the filling area. I walked up to the front. Eddie was sitting down at the counter. I said, "Can I get some air when you get a chance?" Eddie said, "Sure." We walked back to the filling area. Eddie filled the tanks. I said, "Thanks Eddie." I loaded the tanks in the car and drove home.

Saturday ...

David called and said, "We still going diving tomorrow?" I said, "Yeah you want to go to Redondo right?" David said, "Yeah." I said, "Okay but let's do two day dives so I can recuperate from the shark." David said, "Okay." I said, "I bought a dive camera. I'll bring it. I also got my new dive light and dive knife." David said, "Good sounds like you're ready to do some deep night dives." I said, "We'll see."

Sunday morning ...

I called David and asked him if he was about ready. He said he was and would be over in a few minutes. I loaded my dive gear in the car. David drove up and loaded his. We were on our way to Redondo. I said, "That was so much fun on the three day boat trip. They treat you so good. We did a lot of diving, eating and I slept good. At night they pull the boat into coves. I didn't feel the boat move at all when I was sleeping." David said, "Let me know next time you go and I'll go too." I said, "Okay. Lee's been coming over too. I hate taking him back home. I don't care much for it over there. I think I'm going to ask him to spend the night, not take him back and see what happens." David said, "Give me a call if you need anything and I'll help you if I can." I said, "Okay. How about an egg biscuit for breakfast?" David said, "Sounds good to me."

We drove through the drive through, got our food then drove to Redondo and parked. There were a few dive instructors and trainees in the parking lot but not many. We sat in the car and started eating. I looked out toward the ocean and said, "Man that was a big shark and it was right there. Right off the beach. Look at those people swimming out there. They don't have any idea that there could be a shark that big that close to shore." David said, "I wouldn't have thought they would come in that close either. They must eat out there in the canyon and come in close at night to sleep." I said, "That's weird isn't it? I still can't believe that you went next to it all the way to its head then shined your dive light in its eye and woke it up. I bet you're the only person that's ever done that." David said, "I wasn't worried until I realized it was a shark." I said, "When you jumped back, that's when I panicked and started going in as fast as I could." David said, "I know I could barely keep up with you."

We finished eating and got out of the car. David walked over to the sign at the entrance of the parking lot and started looking at. He walked back and said, "The sign says you can't come in after 10:00 PM but if you're already in it's okay to stay past 10:00 PM. So we didn't have to hurry after all." I said, "We didn't. I bet we wouldn't have seen the shark if we weren't hurrying. I bet it would have heard us and swam off but since we were going so fast we snuck up on it." David said, "I bet you're right."

We unloaded our dive gear and put it together. I put a disposable camera in the camera housing, attached the strobe onto it and put the corrective lens on. I said, "If you see anything good let me know and I'll take its picture." David said, "Okay."

We started putting our wetsuits on. I said, "What do you think about our dive plan being to go out and come back?" David said, "Sounds like a good dive plan to me." I said, "Yeah and you navigate." David said, "Okay." I walked over and helped David with his hood.

We put our dive gear on, walked across the parking lot, down the steps and across the beach to the water. We aired up our BC's, got in, put our fins on and started kicking out.

David looked down toward the end of the pier and said, "You about ready?" I said, "I'm as ready as I'll ever be. The last time we were here I didn't think I would ever get in this water again." David said, "Yeah it was a lot of fun, wasn't it?" I said, "It was exciting. I hope this dive is boring. I'll meet you on the bottom." David said, "Okay." We put our mask on, our regulators in our mouths and started letting the air out of our BC's. We were going down.

We were on the bottom. We started going out at a slow pace. We got to the drop off and stopped. We looked down it and I took some pictures of it. I then took some of David. He looked at me like don't waste the film. I gave David the okay signal. He gave it back. We slowly started down the drop off. We got to the bottom of it and slowly started going out. The visibility was good. We kept going slowly while looking around. I kept my eyes wide open with my head moving back and forth looking around everywhere. I thought I know they're out here somewhere but I kept telling myself they're not here, it's daytime, don't worry, breathe slow and relax. We started gradually picking up speed and going faster.

I checked our depth. We were at a hundred and five feet. We weren't seeing anything, I kept thinking to myself, "Good I don't want to see anything!" We speeded up to our normal fast pace. David started pointing for us to turn right so we turned. I checked our depth. We were at a hundred and twenty eight feet. We kept going fast. David started pointing for us to turn right again. We turned and headed in. I thought oh good we're on our way in and we haven't seen anything, no excitement at all! Oh! This is fun. A bat ray was in front of us and started swimming off. I started taking pictures of it. I kept taking pictures until I was out of film. It gradually swam out of sight.

We could see the bottom of the drop off coming up. We went up to it and went up it. We went over the top of the drop off and started going across the sandy bottom still going at our fast pace. We were at eighteen feet. My air was down to four hundred pounds. I pointed up to David. He gave me the okay signal. We went up, aired up our BC's, took our regulators out of our mouths and our mask off.

I said, "That wasn't bad. I was low on air. I only had four hundred pounds." David said, "That's what I had too. We were only at eighteen feet so I was going to see if I could make it all the way in before running out of air." I said, "I should have done that too. I got some pictures but we sure didn't see much." David said, "You never see much in the daytime. It's so much better at night."

We kicked in close, took our fins off, got out and walked up to the showers. We rinsed off, walked up the steps to the car and took off our dive gear then changed tanks. David said, "I hope we see more on the next dive." I said, "Not me. That dive was so nice."

I put a new camera in the housing. We sat around and talked for awhile then David checked his computer and said, "The computer is showing we're ready." I said, "I'm ready when you are." David said, "I'm ready."

We put our dive gear back on. I grabbed the camera. We walked across the parking lot and down the steps. David said, "Let's go down some toward the pier this time and see what's down there." I said, "Okay, but we don't want to get too close." David said, "Yeah. We should probably stay a little way away from where they're fishing at." I said, "Yeah I would hate to get hooked."

We walked down the beach toward the pier. I said, "We sure are getting close." David said, "This should be good here." David checked his compass. We aired up our BC's. I said, "Our dive plan the same - go out and come back." David said, "Yeah." We got in the water, put our fins on and started kicking out. We were looking at the pier as we were kicking out next to it. I said, "I wonder what it's like under the pier." David said, "I don't know but I don't think I would want to go under it. I think it's illegal anyway." I said, "I sure don't want to go under it."

We were even with the end of the pier. I said, "Look at those people fishing. I hope they can't hit us." David said, "I don't think they can. Are you about ready?" I said, "I'm ready. I'll meet you on the bottom." David said, "Okay." We put our mask on, our regulators in our mouths and started letting the air out of our BC's. We were slowly going down.

We were on the bottom. We gave each other the okay signal and started going. We weren't going very fast. We came up to the drop off and slowed down real slow then went over it. It was different here, it wasn't very steep at all.

We got to the bottom of the drop off and started going out. The bottom was different here too. It was still flat but wavy like small hills and valleys. We kept going out looking around. We started picking up speed. We were getting deeper but not very much. We were going along at our normal fast pace. We kept looking around but we weren't seeing much, just a dirt bottom. I had the camera ready just in case. We were at seventy-five feet.

We kept going out. I thought David would probably want to turn left soon and go over some before going back in but we kept going straight out at our fast pace. We were at eighty-three feet. David looked over at me and started pointing to the right then started turning right. I turned with him and thought what is he doing, this is the wrong way. I started getting really nervous. I started breathing deep and fast. I was thinking when we head in we'll be headed straight at the pier.

We kept going at our normal fast pace. David looked over at me and started pointing to the right. We started turning right again. We turned and now we're headed in straight toward the pier. We kept going at our normal fast pace.

I thought oh man we've got to be real close to the pier by now. We kept going fast and straight in toward the pier. I'm so nervous I can barely stand it. I'm really breathing deep fast breaths. I signaled to David for us to turn right. David pointed at an angle for us to only veer to the right a little bit. We turned a little and kept going at our normal fast pace. I thought I hope he turned us enough so we'll miss the pier and all the fishing lines.

We got to the bottom of the drop off. David started pointing for us to turn right and go along the bottom of the drop off away from the pier. I thought oh I would be happy to. We turned and started going along the bottom of the drop off. I was down to eight hundred pounds.

I pointed in to David. David gave me the okay signal. We turned and went up the drop off then started going across the sandy bottom toward shore. I checked my air. I only had three hundred pounds. We were at seventeen feet.

We kept going in fast. I pointed up to David. We went up, aired up our BC's, took our regulators out of our mouths and our mask off. I said, "I thought I would make it but my needle was barely off zero." David said, "That's about where mine was." I said, "I got really nervous around the end of the pier." David said, "Yeah I didn't want to get too close to it." I said, "I thought you were going to run us into it when you turned right. I was expecting to turn left." David said, "I wanted to see what was over there. You sure don't see anything in the daytime. I like it right around dark when it's feeding time better. That's when we saw the shark." I said, "It is a lot more scary at night." We started kicking in. We weren't out very far.

We kicked in close, took our fins off, got out, walked to the showers and rinsed off. I turned around and looked out at the ocean and the people on the beach. I said, "They're out there David, they're out there, right there." David looked at me and said, "What do you think about next time going at feeding time." I said, "Okay. I think I'm ready for it."

Deb, David and I kept on diving. Deb and I would go slow, taking our time, closely looking at everything. David and I would go as fast and as far as we could. Deb and I never did see any large sharks, David and I saw two more.

978-0-595-42939-4
0-595-42939-4